DATE DUE

NO 18 98			
NO 28 00			
JE 4 02			
JE 11 03			
JE 8 05			

DEMCO 38-296

R

FEMALE GANG PARTICIPATION
*The Role of African-American Women
in the Informal Drug Economy
and Gang Activities*

Deborah Burris-Kitchen

Women's Studies
Volume 17

The Edwin Mellen Press
Lewiston/Queenston/Lampeter

Library of Congress Cataloging-in-Publication Data

ISBN 0-7734-8617-8

This is volume 17 in the continuing series
Women's Studies
Volume 17   ISBN 0-7734-8617-8
WS Series ISBN 0-88946-118-X

A CIP catalog record for this book is available from the British Library.

The Edwin Mellen Press   The Edwin Mellen Press
Box 450   Box 67
Lewiston, New York   Queenston, Ontario
USA 14092-0450   CANADA L0S 1L0

The Edwin Mellen Press, Ltd.
Lampeter, Dyfed, Wales
UNITED KINGDOM SA48 7DY

Printed in the United States of America

TABLE OF CONTENTS

ACKNOWLEDGMENTS

I would like to start by thanking my husband Rick for being so patient and understanding. He has been very supportive and I could not have done it without him. I would like to thank my mother and father for their support and understanding. It is important to have loving parents who stand behind you when times get tough. Finally, I would like to thank my colleagues for their mentoring and support. Thank you Doug Davidson, Ron Kramer, Stan Robin, Alan Jacobs, and Sharon Davis.

Deborah Burris-Kitchen

PREFACE

By Douglas V. Davidson
Western Michigan University, Department of Sociology

The sample population and the topics investigated are the subjects of intense debate in the scholarly and popular literature. The lifeways of young urban inner city African-American women entangled in what E.F. Frazier and later Daniel P. Moynihan have referred to as the "tangle of pathology" described in terms of welfare dependence, single parenthood, deteriorating housing, drug infested neighborhoods, and widespread gang violence are the subjects of numerous scholarly treatments as well as political debates. For the most part, the scholarly works are based on secondary analyses of census generated data. The political debates use the scholarly works as the bases for the various policy options proffered to resolve the complex problems of the inner city underclass.

In the midst of this "hue and cry," one rarely hears the voices of the people who are the subjects of these discussions. Thus the research conducted for this monograph is a refreshing and informative contribution. It is a study of young African-American women residents of a middle-class midwestern city. The investigator was attempting to determine if these young women were aware of the existence of female-headed gangs or drug distributing "crews." Earlier research studies conducted in a large midwestern city reported the presence of both female headed gangs and drug dealing crews. In addition, the investigator was interested in how these young women constructed their lives and to what extent their experiences affirmed the prevailing images portrayed in the scholarly and popular literatures. As one would expect, the search for informants was difficult. However, with the assistance of a friend who served as an intermediary, she was able to locate her sample informants. Given the racial tension prevalent in our society, locating black female inner city youths willing to grant an interview with a white female social scientist on such sensitive subject matters as gang activity, drug distribution, racism, attitudes toward the police, etc. is not a small task.

The result is an informative study which creatively combines the insights of feminist theory, black women studies, sociological and criminological theory to analyze and interpret the responses she received. Using feminist inspired methods of inquiry, she allowed her respondents to set the tone and direction of the interviews. While she had certain questions formulated, she interjected these where it seemed appropriate. In essence, the interviews were more conversational in tone than tightly constructed formal social science interviews. The information obtained or shared reflects the nature of the relationship she was able to establish with the informants; her ability to establish trust and confidence. It appears that she was quite successful in this approach in that the responses are indepth, insightful, and have an authentic quality.

The message contained in the responses will corroborate some of the existing generalizations and challenge others. One of the most outstanding qualities of the responses is the sophistication and the intelligence of the respondents. They were outstanding representatives of the larger population. I was impressed with their sense of consciousness and awareness of dominant societal factors contributing to the conditions impacting their lives as well as the internal African-American cultural values and practices which can be barriers or obstacles to achieving desired goals, or sources of inspiration and sustenance in their efforts to transcend the limitations of their environment. Equally impressive are the expressions of pain, anger, resilience, humor, and a sense of hope in spite of the bleakness of the current economic landscape.

While the study has such to offer policy-makers, it will not make their tasks easier. The responses describe a community in the throes of a variety of problems emanating from the historical damages of a slavery and compounded by the consequences of the deindustrialization plaguing large and middle-sized cities. The current proposed reforms in the welfare system do not appear to be the solution in that no one can see how the "new" jobs will provide enough income to cover living expenses and health care benefits. The same can be said about the so-called "war on drugs." If intensified efforts are made to reduce and/or eliminate their sale and distribution, what will the government do to replace this source of illicit income? As the respondents indicate, that income is often vital to the survival of many inner city residents.

These young women share their world in an open and honest manner. There is much we can learn from the experiences expressed herein. The wisdom manifest in their discourse reveal most poignantly the cost of poverty and repressed opportunities. One cannot help but wonder what their contributions would be if they had the opportunity to develop their potential to its fullest. We must find ways to cease this waste of our most important resource—the minds and creative abilities of our people.

SISTERS IN THE HOOD

Deborah Burris-Kitchen, Ph.D.

University of LaVerne

This research assembles and organizes the literature in the areas of African-Ame women, the political economy of racism, the Black feminization of poverty, drug use distribution, and gang violence. This dissertation explores extant theoretical approaches a special emphasis on their relationship to the underground economy. The researcher ethnographic methods to examine the role that female gang members play in the under drug infested community of south central Fort Wayne, Indiana. Of the Black fen interviewed, some were drug dealers, others were using illegal drugs, and still others females who just found themselves in the inner-city, in the middle of these drug dealing war zones.

A major finding of the research is that race and class are salient factors in determ gang involvement. Because Black women are one of the most oppressed groups iı United States, they too are entering the informal economy to make money in a society v access to making real money has been denied them. As Black women enter the info economy, they too will be victims and perpetrators of violent offenses which are an intr part of the informal economy. The research reveals that underclass Black women ı variety of economic means to meet the survival needs of their family. Thus, selling d prostitution and welfare are often combined to support their children. These Black wc appear to be assuming many of the attitudes and behaviors hither to associated with n exclusively.

LIST OF TABLES

CHAPTER I

INTRODUCTION

Look at my arms! I have ploughed and planted and gathered into barns, and no man could head me—and ain't I a woman? I would work as much and eat as much as a man—when I could get it—and bear the lash as well! and ain't I a woman? I have born thirteen children and seen most of them sold into slavery, and when I cried out with my mother's grief, none but Jesus heard me—and ain't I a woman? (Hooks, 1981, pp. 159-160).

Although Sojourner Truth gave this very powerful speech as early as 1851 at a Women's Rights Conference, many Sociologists still fail to note the differences between the White female and Black female experiences (MacKinnon, 1982; West, 1988). Most White feminists research focuses on the issues facing White women, and use the term Black as an intensifier of the female experience (to be disadvantaged because you are female, but only more so). These theorists have been criticized for their gender essentialist approach to studying Black female experiences (Harris, 1990). While still other theorists have seen the African-American female experience as different because of the Black matriarchy, pathology and the deterioration of the Black family (Moyers, 1986; Moynihan, 1965). These theorists were critical of the African-American female and the African-American family because it was culturally different from the traditional White-European family structure. However, to compare Black women to White women or to Black men neglects a view of the African-American female experience as one of a woman and as a person of color. The essays and poems in *This Bridge Called My Back* (Moraga & Anzaldna, 1981) describe experiences of women of color and illustrate how radically different they are from White women or Black men. Some articles are written by those coming from the underclass which links class issues to the writings of Black feminists.

This research project is significant because it will enable us to incorporate, along with feminists literature, the experiences of African-American female gang members. In the past it appears that female gang members have been appendages of male gangs. Although there have been few accounts of female gang activity, a sociohistorical approach to past and current research on female gangs suggested that female gang members are exercising greater independence, where it may parallel the development of greater independence of African-American women in the formal economy. Female gang members (specifically African-Americans) are aggressively gaining their economic independence which may extend from the previous cultural phenomenon embodied in the African-American female heritage. Unlike White females, Black females have never had the opportunity to act out the docile, dependent, fragile stereotypical White female role, as reflected in the Sojourner Truth's passage at the beginning of this article. However, gang research has indicated that African-American female gang members did not exercise as much independence and aggression in the late 1970s and through the 1980s as they do today. It appears that there is a feminist movement of sorts occurring within the informal economy which may parallel those of the feminist movements in the formal economy.

The informal economy, according to Jaffee (1990), is made up of "street vendors, peddlers, and hucksters who offer goods and services to the urban cash market" (p. 60). Jaffee goes on to explain how the informal economy is a functional element of the formal economy. The intense competition lowers prices, because items can be sold cheap in the informal economy. Also, the informal economy acts as a reserve labor force for the underemployed and unemployed. "The informal sector serves as a huge reserve army of unemployed and underemployed labor that weakens the bargaining position of the formal-sector workers and drives down wages" (Jaffee, 1990, p. 60). Thus, the concept of the informal sector should encompass any economic activity that operates outside the definition of the formal economy (Portes & Walton, 1981). Hence the informal sector, for the purpose of this research, includes all economic activity that is not included in the formal sector (i.e. jobs where employees are paid under the table in cash, and illegal economic activities such as selling drugs, prostitution, gambling, etc.). These are all activities included in the informal economy because they are employment opportunities that are not included as part of the GNP or tax base of the United States. These economic sectors operate outside wall-street.

It is also important to explore how the women's lives are different by looking at the forms of survival they have chosen. Possibly the informal economy may be seen as the only alternative to welfare and poverty. It is within this informal economy that the laissez-faire, dog-eat-dog, struggle inherent in capitalism plays itself out.

Therefore, it is also important to look at the economic condition of African-American women. The objective of this research will be to look at how these women are constructing their lives and connect it with the various economic and feminist literatures.

CHAPTER II

Literature Review: Introduction

The literature review will attempt to connect and integrate feminist literature, political economy literature on women in the work force, and gang research, in order to explain the distinctive features of female corporate gang members, and their attempt to gain their economic independence aggressively in an economic system which relegates African-American women to poverty and welfare, as presented in Wilson's (1987) book entitled *The Truly Disadvantaged.*

CHAPTER III

The History of Racial and Gender Oppression

When a society transforms from a subsistence economy to a capitalist economy, the traditional age-sex-race hierarchy becomes an age-sex-race and class hierarchy. Depending on the composition of the society, the segmental order in which sex and race interact varies. For example, in a culture without a dominant ethnic group, or with only one ethnic group, gender would evolve as the most salient component of discrimination. However, if one ethnic group, or race is dominant over another, as in the United States, race becomes the most salient intricacy. African-American women are victims of race, class and gender oppression, but race becomes the major determinant of social status, gender becomes a secondary issue.

During the period of slavery African-American women, outside of their ability to reproduce the work force, were viewed as genderless, outside of sexual oppression, by slave owners. African-American women worked alongside their male counter-parts in the cotton fields, tobacco factories, the rice mills and sugar refineries. The Black woman's master demanded her to be as masculine as men at her work. A majority of the slave woman's work was seen as taboo by the standards of the 19th century womanhood. According to Davis (1944/1981), a traveler during that period observed a slave crew in Mississippi returning home from the fields and described the group as including . . .forty of the largest and strongest women I have ever saw together, they were all in a simple uniform dress of a bluish check stuff, their legs and feet were bare, they carried themselves loftily, each having a hoe over their shoulder, and each walking with a free powerful swing like chasseurs on the march. (p. 11).

For the Black women during slavery, domestic work, within their own families, was the only meaningful work which was not controlled by their oppressor. While there was no pay for household work, the African-American woman ensured a sense of autonomy for herself and her men through this type of work. This made her role far more important than the father's in the Black family. According to Davis (1944/1981)

the black woman in chains could help lay the foundation for some degree of autonomy, both for herself and her men. Even as she was suffering under her unique oppression as female, she was thrust into the center of the slave community. She was, therefore, essential to the survival of the community. (p. 17)

African-American women were often responsible for defending their men against the slave system's attempts to demean them. They knew the importance of having strong male role models for their young boys, because if their men were being degraded, so too were their sons, and the entire Black community. Most Black women enjoyed equality with their Black male counterparts, because of their position of being equally oppressed in the work force, and their strength and support within the slave family. Black women often joined revolts against slavery and work stoppages alongside their male equals. "Black women were equal to their men in the oppression they suffered; they were their men's social equals within the slave community; and they resisted slavery with a passion equal to their men's" (Davis, 1944/1981, p. 21).

Following the Civil War, a time which promised freedom for Blacks, both male and female, was a time when racism ran deepest in the United States. Even though on paper slaves were free, Blacks were still not accepted in either the north or the south. It was the Black woman, especially in the south, who felt the greatest impact of this, racist, male dominated society. It was during this time period in which Anna Julia Cooper wrote her book entitled *A Voice from the South*. She realized, like the slave mothers before her, that women in the Black Community would be responsible for the liberation of their young. She felt this liberation would be best achieved through the education of her race. Education would allow Black women to organize social movements for justice, equality and freedom for all. She realized that women as mothers were the first trainers, teachers and educators from the moment they birthed their children. She goes on to suggest that Black women must take on the role of teacher, homemaker, wife, mother and missionary. Up to that point in history, society had done very little to provide Blacks with an education. Society had managed to even restrict African-Americans to positions that required little education, low pay and low self-esteem. This was especially true for the free African-American female (Cooper, 1892/1988).

About the same time Anna Julia Cooper was writing, U.S. society's attitudes and technology were drifting toward an expansionist foreign policy and imperialism. "Cuba, the Philippines, Hawaii, several smaller islands, and much of Central and South America came within the sphere of influence as America became an important factor in world affairs" (Leiman, 1993, p. 66). U.S. industrialists were opening up their markets and using their political and economic powers to access less expensive and new raw materials as well as increasing their buying population to invest and augment new profits. "The lesson of imperialism for American blacks is that a society willing to exploit `backward' colored people in less developed countries could not be expected to espouse democracy for its own `backward' people" (Leiman, 1993, p. 67). This view of Blacks as inferior was a dominant ideology of whites in all classes and all political realms in America (Leiman, 1993). This industrialist, imperialist, mentality, coupled with male supremacy left Black women in a unique position politically and economically; they were now moved to the bottom of the social class hierarchy even within their own families.

This so called, new found freedom for Black males, afforded to them by the ending of slavery, became a new form of slavery for Black females. The male dominated society dictated a new position for Black females in Black communities. Even when moving north, Blacks, both male and females, had to take very low paying jobs, this left the female alone to raise her family, while raising the families of the White women (those Black women who were employed as housekeepers also provided child care for the wealthy White women). Most Africa-Americans migrated to the north where they were forced to, and in some ways still do, live in areas recently labelled ghettos. Even if Black women did not grow up in ghetto areas, they were constrained by the same boundaries of freedom as their ghetto sisters (Leiman, 1993).

Wallace (1990) stated the following:

Although I didn't grow up poor and I went to private schools, I did grow up in Harlem. But whether a black woman who desires to be an intellectual or a writer or an artist grows up poor or in Harlem or not, there is, I think, a `Harlem' of the mind set that may set the parameters of her endeavors. In particular, the idea that the black community has little need for certain levels of intellectual activity is as compelling among many black women of the middle class as it is among black women of the working or so-called `underclass' (those who have fallen into the `black' market economy of drugs and AFDC). (p. 6)

When Michelle Wallace entered grade school, she was asked what she wanted to be when she grew up. She blurted out, not thinking, "I want to be the President." By the time she was in Junior High, she had conceded to being the President's wife. It was not until much later that she realized that she couldn't even be the first lady, because she was a Black woman. According to Wallace (1990), African-American women are still today silenced as a group, and deprived of their dreams.

I consider it a cultural crisis of the first order that so few people of color, especially women, are in positions of power and authority in the production of newspapers, books, magazines, television, film, radio, music movies, academic journals and conferences, and university faculty and curricula. (p. 6)

It is amazing that our government and policy-makers can continue to blame inner-city violence on the deterioration of the Black family without acknowledging the special needs of the Black female in the 1990 Presidential Elections. "Black women never came up, even though they might have been considered the object, along with their children, of some of the most repressive social policies in both the Democratic and the Republican parties" (Wallace, 1990, p. 245). How are these women to view themselves in the economic and political realm of the mainstream, when they have been ignored and silenced throughout U.S. history? The frustrations of current economic and political conditions may be one of the many variables contributing to the increasing violence which is a result of the drug culture and the necessary emergence of this informal economy. Many women involved in gang activities, including selling drugs, realize that their options for education and employment are very limited. In the 1990s, conditions of African-American females have not changed in many essential ways from the days when the end of slavery promised a new found freedom for all Blacks.

CHAPTER IV

The History of Drug Use and Drug Distribution

Throughout American history, drug distribution and sales have provided economic alternatives for immigrants who found it difficult to survive within the context of the formal economy. Indeed, well into the 1990s the drug market has remained apart of living in the inner city. As the inner-city neighborhood structure changes, more and more displaced adolescents turn to drugs, not only for monetary security, but the idea of being involved in the selling of drugs provides a degree of purpose, challenges to the otherwise unchallenged youth, along with a sense of identity (Currie, 1989). Young, intelligent, Black females need to be added to the historical emergence of the informal drug economy to make this documentation more complete.

In order to understand better how the African-American fits into the current market of illicit drugs, it is useful to briefly overview the history of the informal drug economy within the United States.

Throughout the 1800s opiates were purchased over the counter. In 1875 San Francisco elites became concerned with the Chinese laborers free usage of opium and outlawed their opium smoke dens. Whites organized to oppress the Chinese labor class from 1875 to 1880 during the onset of the depression. Eventually, in 1909, the Congress enacted the Opium Exclusionary Act, thereby prohibiting importation of opium and its derivatives from China, except for medical purposes (Goode, 1989; Thomas, 1992).

Thomas (1992) lists several reasons why the Chinese were marked for distribution of opium as well as reasons for their behavior being the target of legal sanctions. First, the Chinese immigrants, because of racial hostility, were forced into poverty stricken areas of newly developing cities. By 1890 there were nearly 100,000 Chinese living in red light districts, which also meant that opium usage was another vice offered in these districts (Thomas, 1992). "Secondly, the social upheaval from the massive waves of migration to the cities of the United States and the uneasy mixing of cultures made informal social controls within the family or the original community difficult to enforce" (Thomas, 1992, p. 269). And finally, attitudes toward drinking, along with laws prohibiting drinking, changed the status of many drinkers into users of narcotics (Thomas, 1992).

Eventually, the same racist fears that were previously used against the Chinese and opium, brought about the Harrison Narcotics Act of 1914, which required individuals to register their narcotics use with the Treasury Department. The act was primarily proposed to control the trafficking of narcotics. However, a series of Supreme Court decisions between 1919 and 1922 also made it illegal for physicians to prescribe narcotics to their patients (Goode, 1989; Thomas, 1992).

The Harrison Act witnessed the emergence of a criminal class of addicts and dealers that previously did not exist. The link between addiction and crime was forged. In the 1930s marijuana smokers became the next target or moral censors. Like the link between opium use and the Chinese and the link between African-Americans and narcotics, marijuana use became the drug connected to Mexican-

Americans. Marijuana use was described as a substance which caused Mexican-Americans to become violent (Musto, 1973). The result was the 1937 Marijuana Tax Act which regulated the importation and use of marijuana, and established a criminal class of marijuana users and importers. The possession of marijuana became criminal, not because of a exhaustive examination of the effects of marijuana on humans, but because of persistent racist attitudes toward racial minorities in the United States (Goode, 1989).

By 1951 not only were illegal drug distributing, selling, and using subcultures firmly established in the United States, but Congress was well on its way to suppressing these subcultures. Numerous laws were enacted to increase existing controls over production, distribution and possession of illicit substances. In the 1980s the United States witnessed new efforts by the Federal Government to control illicit drugs. The Congress passed the "Comprehensive Crime Control Act" of 1984 and the "Anti-Drug Abuse Act" of 1986. Each legislation strengthened the already existing drug statutes.

Although we have seen a decline in drug use, which many may argue is a result of these newly established laws and policies, Brown (1990) noted that this decline in drug use may only be occurring in the middle-and upper-class areas, and that the African-American community may be the district paying the highest price for the interdiction approach. He went on to state that

> the black community has paid an unconscionably high price for the 'war on drugs' while deriving few benefits from it. Demand for reduction through interdiction and education may have occurred in more favored sectors of society. However, claims of a decline in drug use among middle class and suburban citizens contrast sharply with signs of increased drug abuse in America's inner cities. (p. 83)

The cost can be measured by the numbers of young African-American males in prisons, young African-American males and females in hospitals and cemeteries due to the AIDS virus passed on through intravenous drug use, and the number of young African-American males dead due to the intrinsic violence which is part of the drug using and distributing world (Brown, 1990). Also, the war on drugs has done little to help the plight of the users and sellers in export countries. More deaths have resulted from the introduction of the war on drugs than ever before.

However horrifying the losses, these exporting nations have gained great economic power through the growing of coca plants, marijuana, etc. In reality, the illegality of certain drugs has lead to an explosion of an illegal drug market on a global level. This illegal market is subsidizing peripheral and semi-peripheral countries surrounding core-states to which they are indebted (Andreas, 1990).

An article written in *The Economist*, October 8, 1988 stated that

> ever since Latin America's debt saga began in 1982, bankers have paid great attention to the ability of debtor countries to boost foreign-exchange earnings so they could service their debts. Although coca dollars have had a big effect, they are nearly always ignored in economic analyses there is little doubt that coca dollars have helped all three countries (Peru, Bolivia, Colombia) cope with balance of payments problems and, thus, foreign debts. (p. 17)

Bolivia estimates that over 70,000 families are supported by the growing of coca plants. In a country with only 6.5 million people this is a very important economic base. The consumers of this cocaine (70%) are residents of the United States (Martin & Romano, 1992). The increase in economic stability in the aforementioned countries, leads to an increase in the ability to pay back debts to core-states. Thus, "the U.S. drug control campaign is not only a low priority but a contradictory objective for Peru (and other economically dependent countries) in the context of the economic crisis and dependence on coca revenues" (Andreas, 1990, p. 365). Also, since 1982, Columbia has paid back its creditors over two billion dollars a year. "In 1988, this was equivalent to about 40% of their export earnings" (Andreas, 1990, p. 365). According to Columbian economist Eduardo Sarmiento, the influx of drug dollars has allowed Columbia to avoid the huge devaluation of currencies experienced by other Latin American countries and reductions in real wages (Andreas, 1990).

The fact that the majority of contemporary immigrants are exiles from nations in the Caribbean and Central America has created favorable conditions for developing markets and amassing wealth in the United States. The Barrios and Ghettos are economically barren terrains and relatively receptive to these new business interests (Kitchen & Davidson, 1993) Indeed, given the long and continuing neglect of these communities, many consider these new opportunities as their best shot for success "American Style" (Kitchen & Davidson, 1993). Thus the observations and linkages made by Martin and Romano (1992) regarding the similarities between the drug economy and prohibition has a substantial affinity with the occurrence in contemporary urban Black, Latino and Asian enclaves (Kitchen & Davidson, 1993).

The existence of Jamaican Posses, Dominican networks, Columbian networks, Peruvian networks, African, Chinese, Vietnamese and other Asians with prior involvement in the traffic is contributing to the wealth, violence, drug addiction and its, sometimes fatal, consequences in underclass, underdeveloped, non-white communities (Kitchen & Davidson, Forthcoming). This could also be contributing to the increasing violence on young African American women in these same underclass communities.

We can place gang violence in the context of the economic and political realms of society. As mentioned earlier, many Second and Third World countries gain economic and political power through the distribution and exportation of drugs. The fact that a majority of contemporary immigrants are exiles from nations in the Carribean, South and Central America, has created favorable conditions for developing markets and amassing great wealth in Barrios and Ghettos in the urban United States (Kitchen, Davidson & Walker, 1994).

Historically, European immigrant groups, through the sales of illegal alcohol products, contributed to the development of organized crime networks. Organized crime networks and groups became very powerful, diversified and institutionalized. What appears to be occurring now is that the new immigrant groups from Latin America, Asia, the Caribbean, and to a lesser extent Africa, may be following the same historical patterns as early immigrants. However, the main product by which these gangs earn their money is through drug trafficking. Organized crime among these new immigrant groups is following the traditional patterns: diversification of criminal and non criminal activities; widespread experience with corruption of public officials; and the quick use of violence for business purposes has become the norm (Kitchen, Davidson & Walker, 1994).

As mentioned earlier, the existence of Jamaican posses, Dominican networks, Colombian networks, Peruvian networks, Chinese, Vietnamese, African and other Asians with prior involvement in the trafficking is contributing to the wealth, violence, drug addiction and its consequences on economically disadvantaged communities. However, some are accumulating large fortunes which are enabling them to make contributions to their communities, helping to support their families, and other family members to college, or invest in legitimate money making opportunities. Intriguing in one way is the fact that this drug wealth, with its power and influence, has provided underclass ethnics with the economic clout that oil did for the Arabs, and electronic technology did for the Japanese. These economically impoverished African-Americans can establish their economic niche in the United States through the investment derived from these drug profits (Kitchen, Davidson & Walker, 1994). However, in underclass communities, the organized groups that distribute and sell drugs are called gangs, rather that being labelled as part of the organized crime ring.

The type of gangs that I am interested in are similar to the ones that Carl Taylor labels corporate gangs. This type of gang, according to Taylor (1993), is designed and maintained for the sole purpose of producing revenue in a capitalist underground economy. This is the type of gang I believe will yield the best data for determining how women are gaining their economic independence in an underground capitalist system. "This gang type is well organized for specific objectives and goals. The bond for this gang is not comradeship nor socialization of its members, but financial gain by criminal actions" (Taylor, 1993, p. 19).

CHAPTER V

The History of the Black Feminization of Poverty

According to Margaret Simms (1985), the Black families headed by females have the highest rates of poverty of any other family in the United States, with the exception of Hispanic families. This has made these women disproportionately dependent on welfare and less likely to receive support from absent fathers. This has not only become a significant problem for Black females, but for the African-American community in general. Using 1984 as a basis of comparison, 50% of Black families with children were run by single women. A number of theories have been suggested to explain this phenomenon. Many discuss factors such as the male-female sex ratio, high unemployment of Black males, and opportunities to collect welfare. "About one-half of out-of-wedlock births among Blacks are to women under the age of 20. These women are least likely to have job skills and educational attainment necessary to generate incomes above the poverty level" (Simms, 1985, p. 142). This results in poorer opportunities and health conditions for their children as well. More recently, Leonard Harris (1992) notes that "Women in the underclass are twice as likely as men to be jobless; men in the underclass are more likely to be imprisoned than men in any other class" (Harris, 1990, p. 34). Thus, the economic oppression of Black males contributes to the large number of unemployed and underemployed men in underclass communities.

In 1983 the average annual income for a Black female-headed household was $7,999.00. This figure is about 60% that of White female-headed households. Female-headed households comprise two-thirds of all Black families living below the poverty level. "While poverty rates are very high among Black families with an adult male present, Black families headed by a woman are three times as likely to be poor or near poor" (Simms, 1985, p. 143). Black female-headed households with the woman heading the family being under the age of 24 had a poverty rate of 84% in 1983. And the alleged war on poverty has not changed the conditions of Black female-headed families. The female-headed family seems to be in the same position as they were in 1966, when the war on poverty began (Simms, 1985).

More recently, Lawson reports: "According to government figures, 30% of all blacks and nearly 50% of all black children live in poverty" (Lawson, 1992, pp. 127-128). The economic conditions of Blacks and Black female-headed households have not changed within the last ten years, since Simms research was published in 1985. The main problem, Lawson explains, is joblessness. Industrial jobs, due to automation, are moving out of the urban areas leaving behind lack of opportunity and marginalized status. "Capital disinvestment and the red-lining polices of banks are among major factors in the material erosion of its social environment" (Lawson, 1992, p. 155). This destruction of a community's ability to reproduce itself materially compels the group to call into question their belief in the norms, practices and meaning of the larger society (Lawson, 1992).

To illustrate that the economic conditions of Black females have not changed over the past decade, I will start by looking at data from the 1980s. As for child support payments, only one-half of the Black female-headed households received child support in the early 1980s. And for those who did receive support, the mean payment was only $1,440.00. Black women who live below the poverty level were the least likely to be receiving support payments. In 1981 only 12.3% of Black mothers living in poverty received support money from the absent fathers (Simms, 1985). Poverty rates are even higher among Black women who work full-time. So even full-time employment does not guarantee a better standard of living for this impoverished group (Simms, 1985).

The feminization of poverty is an important part of the current growth in those who are falling below the poverty level. Not only do Black women experience high rates of unemployment but they also have a difficult time entering the labor market. Blacks, both males and females, experience the largest increases in unemployment during recessions, but fail to reenter the job market at high rates during economic recoveries. Therefore, Black female unemployment is not the only issue facing the impoverished African-American community, but we must also consider the economic conditions of the Black males (Simms, 1985). Perhaps Black males are better off not marrying or staying with their families. It is much more difficult for Black couples to get government support, than for a single female with children.

Also, Black women have not benefitted from access to White men. Black women and their mulatto children have not gained property through inheritance, nor have they had access to marrying White men who are better off economically than their Black male counterparts. Therefore it is difficult for Black females to advance economically from the advantages afforded to them by White male capital and property (Leiman, 1993; Sowell, 1984).

According to Sowell (1984),

> a black woman does not have an opportunity equal to that of a white woman to become the wife of a given white man since white men are on the whole better-off financially than black. One could imagine calculating the monetary damages to black women of this kind of racial discrimination that such a notion strikes most people as absurd is mere testimony for the fact that we all basically accept the legitimacy of the practice of racial discrimination in the intimate, personal sphere. (p. 259)

Huff (1990), noted that between 1970 and 1984 "Black and Hispanic families headed by women increased by 108% and 164%, respectively, compared with an increase of 63% for Whites" (Huff, 1990, p, 228). Out-of-wedlock births for Black teenagers rose 89% between 1970 and 1983. This trend left nearly half of those children from Black female-headed households living in poverty. This brought about a population of truly disadvantaged young who are ill equipped to participate in the dominant society, and who are being denied basic opportunities afforded to them by civil rights advances, or by affirmative action programs. The net effect of historical and contemporary discriminatory practices is the existence of economically disadvantaged groups in the ghettos which contributes to the exodus of those residents who were capable of economic and political success, leaving few role models for those left in the inner-cities (Huff, 1990).

Pamela Sparr (1984) suggests that

> by stressing what is uniquely female, proponents of that argument may leave a mistaken impression that sexism is the fundamental problem. They fail to examine thoroughly the nature of the capitalist economy, which requires and maintains an impoverished class of people. (p. 9)

For the United States the impoverished class of people has continuously been people of color. The economic conditions of Blacks in general makes the family arrangements in the urban ghetto areas female and single parent (Sparr, 1984). Therefore, social scientists need to focus on the economic survival of the African-American community, not just the economic survival of the Black female.

Black women have had to participate in the labor market longer and in greater numbers than their White female counterparts because the economic conditions of Black males required that they contribute economically to the family. Historically, Black women have never been dependent, docile, homemakers, but have been providers for their families. "At every educational level, Black women were more likely to work full time, full year than White women" (Malveaux, 1985, p. 19). However, the Black women who work are more likely to work in traditionally female jobs (service, clerical, and private household work), than White females. Black women are disproportionately represented in areas such as food service, child care and hairdressing. These positions pay wages well below the poverty level for full time work. Sixty-nine percent of all Black women who worked at service jobs full-time, at full-year pay, earned less that $180 per week. "8.2% of Black women service workers employed in `traditionally' `Black female' service jobs earned weekly pay that on a full-time, full-year basis placed them at less than 125% of the poverty line" (Malveaux, 1985, p. 19).

Lieman (1993) also notes the shocking incidence of poverty among Black women. Like his predecessors (Malveaux, 1985; Simms, 1985; Sowell, 1984) he notes the impoverished conditions of the Black female-headed household. His findings show that in 1986 67.1% of all children in Black female-headed households lived below the official poverty level—defined by the Federal Government as 12,675 dollars per year for a non farm family of four. This figure translates into 30.7% of

Black families living below the poverty level as opposed to 10% of the White families. According to Leiman (1993), race remains a very powerful predictor for explaining poverty. However, the gender feature illustrates the phenomenal burden on Black women..

Leiman (1993), also notes, the young Black population is so frustrated with their disproportionately impoverished and marginalized conditions, that they have stopped actively looking for jobs in the legitimate economy, and have begun working, and looking for employment within the informal economy (selling drugs, theft, prostitution and numbers running).

While both Black and White women experience inequality in the labor force, their concerns about economic stability may be very different. The Black women's agenda must address both racial and gender interests. Also while White women may see White men as their oppressors, Black women do not see Black men as oppressors, because Black men have traditionally not been economically stable enough to oppress Black women. Black women must not only be concerned with the economic conditions of their gender, but also with the economic conditions of the Black community. It is this sense of economic deprivation within the entire Black community, coupled with the feminization of poverty, that has led to generation after generation of welfare recipients among Black, female-headed families. The economic conditions of the African-American community, combined with a sense that there is no other alternative to welfare, may be contributing to the increase in Black female participation in corporate gangs. These young women may view their conditions as hopeless and with no legitimate opportunities to escape welfare and poverty, may turn to selling drugs in order to earn the respect which is not given to welfare mothers. And many of these women and girls don't care how violent or aggressive they have to be to get the money.

CHAPTER VI

The Economy and Crime

Gangs and the Informal Drug Economy

Our society, rather than looking at economic conditions, blames the victim for their immoral and unethical behavior, reflecting the complex intersection of race and class privileges; this can be exemplified by examining the rates of imprisonment and victimization. Although black males only make up about 6% of the population, they make up more than 50% of the prison population (Leiman, 1993).

> The reactionary impulse of blaming the victim rather than the capitalist mode of production becomes highly valuable in helping to retrench the welfare state while maintaining the legitimacy of the system. The real objective need of monopoly capital is to maintain class power against a potentially more powerful working class. (p. 183)

African-Americans are overrepresented as victims and perpetrators in all areas of the criminal justice system, with an exception of white collar, governmental, and political crimes, but seldom has institutionalized racism been more clearly illustrated than by the appearance of so many young African-Americans, males and females, on lists naming them as victims or perpetrators of the most brutal violent crime—homicide. While the African-American population only makes up roughly 14% of the U.S. population, they account for 47% of homicide victims. Black Americans are six times more likely than their white counterparts to be victims of homicide. Homicide is the second leading cause of death among 15- to 24-year-old's, but is the leading cause of death for African-Americans in this same age category. "Homicide contributed fully 40% of all deaths among 15- to 24-year-old black Americans in 1988. The proportion of deaths from homicide among whites of the same age was 8 percent" (Messner & Rosenfeld, 1994, p. 29).

For females, the homicide victimization rate for Whites was much lower than their Black female counter-parts. For White females, the lifetime probability rate for being a victim of a homicide was 1 in 447, for Black females it was 1 in 137. "We cannot think of a more alarming set of social indicators in the United States than those measures of risk for lethal violence among black Americans, especially young black males" (Messner & Rosenfeld, 1994, p. 29). Messner and Rosenfeld (1994) also note that homicide arrest rates between blacks and whites closely correspond with the racial differences in the homicide victimization rates. These findings demonstrate the importance of the continuation of studying the impact of being racially disadvantaged in a society with exceptionally high rates of interpersonal violence.

In a society which has been desensitized to violence, devalues human life, with an economic system which requires both winners and losers, one could easily foresee the existence of a dark side to the American Dream. The American Dream, according to Messner and Rosenfeld (1994), encourages an exaggerated emphasis on monetary achievements while devaluing alternative criteria of success; it promotes a preoccupation with the realization of goals while deemphasizing the importance of the ways in which these goals are pursued; and it helps create and sustain social structures with limited capacities to restrain the cultural pressures to disregard legal restraints. (p. 10).

The American Dream generates strong pressures and an urgency to succeed, but without any kind of moralistic values attached to success, or with narrowly defined rules for success, a general consensus of success may be by any means necessary (Messner & Rosenfeld, 1994). Today's gang activity, and other criminal behavior, may be a manifestation of this current philosophy on economic and political achievement.

Recently, gangs have been expanding into cities and rural areas realizing that selling drugs such as crack, marijuana, and PCP can be extremely profitable. Crack has been found to be the number one profit-maker for dealers for two reasons. First, crack has a very high profit margin. In L.A. and other cities crack can bring a return of 300 to 400 percent. Secondly, crack highs are short lived and highly psychologically addictive which creates much repeat business (Beirne & Messerschmidt 1991; Lyman, 1989; Weisheit, 1990). Given the economic return on crack cocaine, and the economic conditions of the urban underclass, it is no wonder that drug distribution and sales looks like an appealing alternative not only to young Black males, but to young Black females who can only see a future of dependence on welfare.

As Wilson's (1993) research points out, the arrest rates for stereotypical female crimes has been declining (prostitution and amateur theft) since the late 1970s, while arrest rates for women involved in drug related crimes has increased 2.56 times. He states that drug arrests are almost twice as high as predicted for men and more than one-half times higher for women. From the beginning of the decade (1980) to its end, the percentage of all male income-productive crime accounted for by drugs alone increased from 21.02% to 32.67% and for women the percentage nearly doubled, moving from 10.95% to 20.34%. (p. 183).

The new criminal opportunities available through drug sales seems to have impacted female criminality more than male criminality. Although females have been traditionally locked out of other male dominated criminal subcultures, they seem to have moved into the world of drug-trafficking with much dexterity (Wilson, 1993). Because drug dealing typically operates out of someone's home, and forms of communications are needed, like telephones, women may have entered into drug distributing simply because in many underclass communities women are the ones who can provide a stable base from which to operate their business. This new commodity has dramatically altered the criminal activity of the underclass, and the arrest rates of this class. "What these changing patterns of crime commission reveal is the shape of the criminal networks within the underclass and the manner in which public policy interacts with them to reproduce class, caste, and gender inequities" (Wilson, 1993, p. 190).

While Jankowski's (1991) research narrowly focused on male gang members, he did an excellent job in laying out the entrepreneurship of corporate gangs. This is the same entrepreneurship that will be looked for among female gang members. While previous gang research found them to be disorganized, lacking moral values, and work ethics, Jankowski's research illustrates a productive, entrepreneurial work that parallels the same plane as other productive members of the legitimate economy (Jankowski, 1991). According to Jankowski (1991), the entrepreneurial spirit is broadly defined as "a desire to organize and manage business interests toward some end that results in the accumulation of capital" (Jankowski, 1991, p. 101). Jankowski (1991) found five attributes in gang members that are entrepreneurial in character or reinforce the entrepreneurial spirit.

First, Jankowski (1991) found that gang members were very competitive and operate under a social Darwinist perspective of survival of the fittest. He also found that the pursuit of profit exempted gang members from ethical codes that constrain business ventures. He quoted Arrow, an eighteen-year-old African American Gang member from New York, to support his observation of the social Darwinist outlook of gang members:

> Hey, man, what do you mean by ethics? Ethics don't pay the bills, money pays the bills, and I'm hustling to get money. There ain't nobody interested in ethics, morality, and all that shit—the basic line is, did you make money or not? Fuck those guys who lose and then complain, everybody knows that if they won and I or somebody else lost they wouldn't be saying nothing. Hey, it's dog eat dog, and if you ain't up to it, you get eaten, simple as that! And look at the corporate businesses, they ain't moral or ethical, they never have been and they ain't about to be either, 'cause they only know that they want money. Since nobody complains about them, nobody will complain about us. (pp. 102-103).

The second entrepreneurial attribute Jankowski (1991) noted was the gang members drive to get money and material possessions. Some people in inner city neighborhoods get it through legitimate work, but gang members realize that they are not going to make the necessary cash to support themselves individually or as family breadwinners working for minimum wage jobs. They think that the only way to get the cash needed and material rewards is by selling dope. Rodney, a sixteen-year-old gang member laughed when an interviewer asked him if he would rather be working in an auto plant like Chrysler. He responded (Taylor, 1990):

Hell, no, the plant is for suckers. My cousin Darren worked at Fords and he thought it was happening. He worked all day. Overtime, all the time for peanut money. Now my boy Jerome he's younger that Darren and he already got two brand new rides. He works when he wants and he's making big money. Factory money ain't no money. Jerome is rolling with the T's. He used to be with us, but he hooked up with Howard at school and got lucky and joined the T's. When your rolling, life is sweet, you can buy anything and folks respect you. Darren told me I could deliver pizza or work at Wendy's [laughing loudly]. Right! for three or four dollars! No way! work your ass to death and you got nothing. Anyway, the plant got lame-ass foremen, some black and some white, telling dudes like me to do this and assign them the worst jobs; ain't nobody telling me shit.

That's why our crew is my thing. I do what I want. When you get with a crew everything works. If you get with the real fellahs like Jerome did, then you get paid like big time action. The T's drive Benzo's `vettes, Renegades, got big paper and all the bitches they want. Now ain't no factory boys catching that all star action, like the T's. If you work in the plant you're making dough for that ass Lee Iacocca. Work eight hours a day is for suckers. Our crew finds something to make doughski. We don't want no bullshit factory jobs, we want rolling money. Me and my homeboys just waiting to get with the T's or the W's so we can get paid in full. (p. 44).

The third entrepreneurial attribute mentioned by Jankowski (1991) was that of status-seeking. Among gang members the best way to attain status is by accumulating large sums of money. By having large amounts of cash, gang members gain status by being generous with their possessions. Money can be easily given away, more so than other types of material possessions. Once a gang member develops a leisurely and comfortable lifestyle, they begin to gain status by being generous with what they have (Jankowski, 1991).

The fourth entrepreneurial attribute is spending an impressive amount of time on planning activities which will bring them fortune and fame, at least have enough money for short term fame. Most gang members spend a lot of time dreaming about great wealth. And finally, gang members are willing to take great risks in order to attain their goals. While younger gang members (between 9-15) don't realize the danger they are putting themselves into, once gang members get older they take calculated risks involving imprisonment, and violence. They realize how dangerous their lifestyle is, but are willing to take the risk in order to make the money. Clarence, a corporate gang member, was asked (Taylor, 1990) how violence affects him:

> Violence is messy. I don't like it. The violence in crew business is necessary, it's just part of business. Now jits like the [S-1], they like violence: beating, messing with any and everybody that causes problems for our crew. I ain't talking about our enforcers, I could come up stinking. Lot of times it's zero action, you know? Zeros like to beast on anybody. We got some zeros in our demolition crew but I stay clear of them. Zeros don't care about nothing. They ain't afraid to die over any stupid thing. At least our Zeros work a niggah cause, the crew say do it. But the Noes got some whacked Zeros. They like to rape babes, beat up people and kill somebody for fun. There's lots of dudes stanking and it ain't nothing for some zero action. Me, I'd rather chill—take it slow and get me some babe and listen to some sounds.

> Now if somebody catch trouble with our beastmasters it's about paper usually. Doughski makes people ill, you know? If somebody messes with your property, then they need to be checked. I don't call that violence, that's just tightening you business up. Mostly, I just count my paper and let the knuckle boys wreck fake people. Every time somebody gets bloody I get real sick to my stomach. Big Paul dogs me because I can't stand bloody things. But them crazy-ass demo-boys like to hurt niggahs. They just like to beast on whoever's around. Our crew enforces when people ill on them. But I think some of them boys would beast on somebody for free. That is why

I stay clear of them. They dangerous if you get on their bad side. (pp. 55-56)

CHAPTER VII

The History of Female Gang Involvement

Until recently research on female gang involvement has been minimal (Brown, 1977; Campbell, 1984; Thrasher, 1927; Whyte 1943). While many of these early researchers claimed that women played minor roles in gangs and primarily operated as auxiliaries of male gangs or as sex objects/partners, many researchers, including Campbell (1984) claim that the studies on the evolution of female gang members have there historical flaws because of the previous lack of concern for African-American female members. Agnes Baro, Criminal Justice Professor at Grand Valley State University (cited in Taylor, 1993) states that

> we know very little about African-American female gangs or about female criminality in general. Much of what we do know comes from a suspect knowledge based not just because it was developed with considerable male bias but because so much of it lacks reference to the actual feelings, socioeconomic circumstances, or daily lives of the women who are studied. The task then is one of gleaning as much as we can from older and mainly ethnographic studies before we construct a new and hopefully, more accurate perspective. (p. 26)

However limited and flawed the data from early female gang membership may be, there have been many contributions to gang literature which can contribute to our understanding of the evolutionary process of female gang membership. Several quotes from gang members from the 1950s and 1960s and historically moving into the 1990s, can give us a better understanding of what Prothrow (1991) and Fishman (1988) argued in their studies on female gang members. They found that female gang members have become more aggressive, violent and oriented toward `male' crimes. They believe that the economic conditions for underclass African-Americans have forced these women into these roles. The continuous generational chain of poverty has left these women with few alternatives and many operate as a motive for entrance into the illegitimate economy which may parallel those motives that drive males of the same race into the informal market.

Early gang research by Campbell (1984) and Sifakis (1987) depicted the position of women in gangs. A quote from Campbell's (1984) classic study of female gang members from the West side of Detroit in the 1950s illustrates what the role of women was, at least among female gang members who called themselves the Shakerettes.

As quoted in Taylor (1993),

well it's really lots different today, you can't compare our gangs with these young jits today. In the Shakerettes we knew the gang boys as brothers, boyfriends, cousins, friends, before the gang. Were we sexually active? Yeah, some girls were with the boys in gangs, others had boyfriends outside the Shakers. See, girls in a way belong to the gang, we all hung out together or knew everybody from your street. The gang, as far as the girls, was our own thing under the boys. We carry things for `em, things like cigarettes, weapons, wine, or when the stole something and we had to walk or go a long way and they think we might get caught, we would carry or hide their things. We just help anyway the boys would need us. Now sometimes we would fight each other over boyfriends, that happened a lot. (pp. 32-33)

Elanor, 45 talks about her gang life (Taylor, 1993).

I got pregnant when I was thirteen. This counselor at school, a Mrs. Jenkins, tried to steer me right, but it was useless. She told me that Williams was too old and experienced for me. But I wouldn't listen and just said she was stupid. Me, my sisters and cousins, were the Jackie Girls. We called ourselves that after Jackie Wilson, he was so fine, the man was like nothing else, we loved us some Jackie Wilson. Mrs. Jenkins tried to tell me that Willie had babies all over town, but I was in love, my momma couldn't do shit with me. Now my grandmother was strict, but I just used my momma to overrule her. If my grand had been in charge, well, things would have been different. I really thought that William was in love with me, we was gonna get married, right, married. That fool left me the day I told him I was pregnant. I cried and my girls cried, I listen to "Lonely Tear Drops" by Jackie and would cry more.

Today, it's different with these young kids. My girls is tough, and my boys are gangsters. I don't like it, but what can you do? My daughters would never take the shit I took off men. These girls are more ready to get what they want. You ask if I am proud of my girls and their posse? Yeah, it's nice to see them so sure of themselves, and it's nice to know that they ain't gonna make the same mistakes. They don't smoke, drink, and they ain't on no drugs. My girls don't want no welfare, they just like the boy gangsters. They're ready to make it on their own terms, they know what welfare and white people got waiting for them, nothing but shit and grief, that's all. (pp. 39-40)

Other gang and delinquency research which was conducted prior to the emergence or distinction of large corporate gangs (Bowker, Gross & Klien, 1980; Bowker & Klien, 1983; Miller, 1973; Rice, 1963) supports the position that most women gang members were auxiliary members or sexual partners of male gang members. These female members were not nearly as violent and aggressive as today's female gang members.

Rice (1963) found that female gang members could do nothing to gain the type of power and prestige afforded to male gang members. If the girls would get involved in fights, they would be viewed as deviant. If these girls would act to feminine, the male gang members would exploit them as sexual objects.

Miller (1973) found during his investigation of the Molls, that most of the female Molls committed only acts of truancy and theft. The things that these girls stole however were minor in comparison to what the male members were stealing. For example, "girls stole postcards, magazines, popcorn and fountain pens from local stores" (Miller, 1973, pp. ??). Some other girls were caught stealing money and clothing, but most theft was insignificant compared to their male counterparts (Miller, 1973). Miller also found that the female Molls involvement in assaultive behavior was rare (Miller, 1973).

Unlike today, Bowker, gross and Klien (1980), found that female gang members were excluded from participating in planning activities, which supported the hypothesis of the senior author that "one of the latent functions of male delinquent gangs is to facilitate exclusion of females from planning and carrying out those activities that are significantly status confirming" (Bowker, Gross & Klien, 1980, p. 517). However, the authors caution this interpretation since most interviews were take from male gang members. This may only be the way male gang members perceive the roll of women.

Recent studies on female gang activities indicate that women have become more involved in violent, aggressive activities, and have begun to develop their own organizations where they are now the sellers, distributors, and protectors of their own drug markets (Taylor, 1993). This transition of female gang members from caretakers of male members may be a direct result of the economic conditions facing women of color in the United States.

Bowker and Klien (1983), concluded that

> the overwhelming impact of racism, sexism, poverty and limited opportunity structures is likely to be so important in determining the gang membership and juvenile delinquency of women and girls in urban ghettos that personality variables, relations with parents, and problems associated with heterosexual behavior play a relatively minor role in determining gang membership and juvenile delinquency. (pp. 750-751)

Since the emergence of the corporate gang, which mostly revolves around the sale and distribution of crack, few researchers have devoted a significant amount of time to the current roles of female gang members (Anderson, 1990; Huff, 1990; Lyman, 1989; Taylor, 1990). Despite the fact that young women have been part of gangs since the early 1800s (Asbury, 1969), contemporary reports on female gang members still tend to focus on their interpersonal relationships with male gang members. Sometimes these contemporary studies devote a full chapter to the role of female gang members, but most only focus on their sexual promiscuity and ignorance of reproduction and birth control. From 1970 through 1989 there has been an effort to interview female gang members themselves, while earlier research only asked the male gang members what they thought about female gang members, as in Thrasher's research (1927) where he found gangs to be overwhelmingly male.

In recent studies, Hispanic girls and women have been the primary object of investigation (Campbell, 1984; Harris, 1988; Horowitz, 1983; Quicker, 1983). Far less attention has been given to African-American female gang membership (Huff, 1990). Due to the existing literature's ambiguous messages about the role of women in gangs, this study attempts to clarify the roles played by African-American female gang members. It is also important to see how these roles have changed over time, especially with the emergence of new corporate gang structure and the opportunity for making vast amounts of money for women.

A classic study on Black female gang participation was conducted by Fisherman (1988), who reanalyzed data on the 1960s Vice Queens in which she found that their roles were that of sex objects, drinking partners, weapon carriers, and lookouts. The females ties to the gang were usually through their relationships with male gang members. While Miller (1975) felt that most female gangs are auxiliaries of male gangs, Brown (1977) found an autonomous gang of females. Thus one of the issues that prompted this research was the need to clarify whether or not female gangs today are operating independently of male groups, or if they are still being considered as auxiliaries. It is also important to investigate the relationship between the expansion of female gangs and the crack business. Are female gangs breaking away from male gangs in order to get their hands on the money that can be made through the crack industry? What role has the underground economy played in the changing structure of female gangs? And, how has the economic conditions of the African-American community fostered the increase in female gang members?

Harris (1988) found that most female gang members select a sexual partner through the ranks of an associated male gangs. Once this partner is chosen, these women are to remain faithful to their partner until the relationship ends. Jealousy and distrust can disrupt gang activity. When fighting, girls most often use fist and knifes while male gang members are more likely to carry and use guns (Campbell, 1984; Harris, 1988). Campbell found (1984) that male gangs are critical for the existence of female gangs and that when both males and females are present, the girls let the boys monopolize the conversation and make the decisions.

Elijah Anderson's (1990) research also focused on the female as being secondary and a sexual partner of male gang members. He devotes a chapter to the sexual codes and family life of street dwellers in which he portrays women as sexual objects of men. He talks bout how during adolescence it is hard for males to control sexual urges. He claims that the women desire commitment and sexual attention, while the males just want to fulfill their sexual desire without babies or commitment. The man, in order to keep status in his community, must make the women appear crazy with desire for him, while all along he knows he is playing her for a fool. The woman, on the other hand, is trying to trap him or trick him into long term commitment. This sometimes results in pregnancy. The woman feels she can trap her man by having his baby. Usually this just makes the man disappear from her life. She hopes that having his baby will compel him to make a long-term commitment, establishing her claim on him.

In Anne Campbell's book (1984) *The Girls in the Gang*, she gives accounts of three types of female gang members in her study of New York City; focusing on individual members in each gang, she found that each member differed in age, background and roles within their gangs. She found the three had in common their chosen involvement in gang membership and involvement with the criminal justice system. One group is called the Five Percenter's. The female role of the Five Percenter's is to be the guardian of the children and the hearth. She goes on to say that,

the separate nature of men and women is an explicit part of the
Nation's philosophy. Not only is the woman's sexuality controlled by
the stigma of cheapness, but her reproductive functions also become
a matter of male decision. Motherhood and womanhood become
almost inseparable and dictates her role in the structure. (p. 245)

Campbell's interviews not only show the importance of male and female
relationships, but she also illustrates how girls in gangs must be tough and ready to
fight. This is a quote from a Turbin Queen.

I'm glad I got a reputation. That way nobody will start with me, you
know. Nobody will fuck with me—they know, you know. They're
going to come out losing. Like all of us, we got reputations. We're
crazy, nobody wants to fight us for that reason—you know. They say,
No man. That girl might stab me or something like that. (p. 262)

Campbell's research was one of the first to move away from studying female gang
members as an extension of male gangs toward an analysis of their sexual
relationships with male gang members. Campbell (1984) found that these female
gangs exist as a subculture embedded in the larger capitalist society where these
women want the American dream. These women and girls are subscribing to the
new female agenda.

No more suffering or poverty. No more lonely, forced independence,
living alone on welfare in a shabby apartment. First, a good husband;
strong but not violent, faithful but manly. Second, well-dressed
children. Third, a beautiful suburban apartment. Later for the
revolution. (p. 267)

Taylor (1990), in his book *Dangerous Society*, also devoted some time to interviewing female gang members. However, Taylor, unlike previous gang researchers, asked women specifically about their corporate gang formation and activities. Taylor asked gang members why they were forming or joining groups. Brenda, and Lynn responded.

Brenda:

Girls throw just like guys. We want paper and respect like the fellahs. All of us were friends and went to school and hung out after school. Me and Lisa are cousins. Diane and Carol live down the street from me. My man is in the [C-2] and was asking me to do this and that for him. Sometimes he paid good and sometimes he pay me like I was a ho, paying me some ho money.

Lisa and her boyfriend started making paper 'cause he was in the crew with my man. Carol used to drive my man's car whenever I needed to go somewhere and I didn't have no license. Now I drive 'cause we got some fake licenses, but usually Carol drives. So, anyway, we were getting paper off and on for little favors and jobs. You know, first everybody on the block was freaking 'cause we were with the [C-2], next we was driving big cars and dressing fresh. It was fun, big fun, it was live. After doing favors, Carol and Diane started talking about us making paper like the fellahs. We were already working like some of the crew guys. Chuckie showed us how to shoot a Mac 10, Uzi, and one 'em was a .357 Magnum. After a while we started seeing all kind of girl crews at parties, basketball games, and at the lady (a night club). (pp. 58-59)

Lynn:

Check it. Crews got paper, rides and def clothes. My sister used to get with older fellahs and try to get paid. She told me, Get it all, Baby, get it all. So that's why we got our own thing. We get paid for being the Woes women and then we get paid for being a crew. It's too sweet. (p. 60)

Taylor's research in 1993 specifically focuses on women, and interviews with women on their relationships and roles in gangs. Interviews with female gang members show an emergence of a female gang member that is just as cut throat in business practices as any male, and will be just as aggressive as any male to protect her commodity and territory. Female gang members indicate that they are rejecting the roles as mere extensions of male gangs, and working for males as drug runners and prostitutes. These females see the only way out of the ghetto life, while keeping their self-respect, is through the creation of their own crews, with their own rules and values. One gang member even specifically mentions that they are not going to collect welfare or turn tricks for money, but they are going to get money in a respectable way. In one set of interviews, members of the Red Gucci Girls were asked if women are making money on the streets? Two girls who were interviewed were: Harriet, 23; and Vellicia, 19.

Harriet:

It's life and some are and some ain't. It's like fellahs in some ways, lots of fellahs out in the street and they starving. Everybody can't get paid, lots of girls are just waiting for somebody to drop that paper on them. Some girls want a guy to take care of them, they just lazy and they think some man is just gonna give them money, that's what makes it tight out here. Girls who will do anything for paper make it bad for all us smart babes. There are starving girls and girls getting stupid monay. The monay is out here. Benzo's Beemers, Jeeps, you name it, and I've seen it right here in the city.

Now you ain't seeing that kind of shit off no ho monay. The babes out in the life are getting paid, lots of monay out here and girls is getting it. I'm getting it on, this crew ain't on welfare! [the girls laugh and give each other high-fives]. Girls that are making large ain't like fellahs. Now, we get our little jewelry, but we ain't wearing no street sign in diamonds like fellahs, guys like to show off too much, guys do shit that's unnecessary. Girls like to save their money; now you got ho's that fuck up their monay, but more girls save and do smart shit rather than buy six, seven cars and go to Vegas and just blow big monay trying to impress their boys. Now skeezers will try to impress you, they will go and fuck up monay and try to open a hair salon every time! But skeezers fuck their way everywhere, so it's tight for them, they don't know nothing but giving up that ass. When fellahs get tired of your pussy, it's good-bye girl, now, it's get the fuck out of my life bitch! Next bitch! So, a girl got to get her own if she is on the know, me and my jammies got our own, and it's stupid dope when you do it this way, no wonder fellahs do it this way, it's straight this way. Fuck being a ho! (p. 97)

Vellicia:

Anybody that says girls ain't getting it on either don't know or is just full of shit. This city got so many girls getting paid it's crazy stupid. The fellahs is making it real large and girls is making it too! Look here, we ain't saying noting 'bout who it is, that ain't happening, not with us. But, all you got to do is look 'round you. How much does it cost to go out to the clubs and drive the rides, dress that way? Monay is large and just because some sucka from out there don't know, don't mean shit to us. Everythang is 'bout monay, we all out here getting it on, making that monay, that's what it's all about and that's what everybody is doing, it's 'bout getting that monay. Some do, and some want to do it, but it's still 'bout the monay! (pp. 97-98).

Taylor (1990) found that these new drug trafficking crews or posses are more specialized, organized and violent than ever before. He claims that "cocaine and crack cocaine have provided goals, jobs, and economic realities that the African-American communities in Detroit had never seen before" (Taylor, 1990, p. 11). Taylor goes on to note that these corporate gangs are being run with the same

militaristic goals of those of the Fortune 500 companies. "Different divisions handle
sales, marketing, distribution, enforcement, and so on" (Taylor, 1990, p. 7). And in
some subsequent research efforts by Taylor (1993), he found that female gang
members are just as organized, violent, and productive as male gangs. These female
gangs even run their own crews and carry weapons. This differs from what we have
seen in earlier research (i.e., Campbell, 1984). The following case studies from
Taylor's book, *Girls, Gangs, Women and Drugs* (1993), demonstrates the
independence and willingness of these 1990s female gang members to use force.
Perhaps the glass ceiling which is a reality for women in the formal economy, is non-
existent in the informal economy. It would be very unusual to see an all Black
female run a corporation within the legitimate market, but Taylor found a crew that
was run by females in Detroit.

Taylor's research (1993) may also suggest that the female gang members,
realizing their communal responsibility, may be saving more money. As Harriett
alluded to in her comment about girls not spending money on diamonds and gold
chains, etc. Terry Williams in *Cocaine Kids* (1989) talks about how the male gang
members and drug dealers had parties at after hours clubs where they flash their dope
and money. For the male gang culture it is important to broadcast their wealth and
dope through conspicuous consumption and reckless spending. The more members
make, the more individuals can give/share with others, this affords group members
much more prestige.

> Anyone who is allowed to enter after-hours clubs has a certain
> amount of status for that reason alone. Once inside, there is a
> competition, a clamoring for attention, which can include lavish
> spending, elegant attire, and generous sharing of cocaine. Those who
> can create these effects most effectively win the respect and envy of

everyone present, if only for an evening. (p. 100)

Terry Williams book (1992), *Crackhouse*, also illustrates that the traditional role of the female gang member is vanishing. Female gang members in his book agree that the picture of young girls doing anything for drugs is inaccurate. However, Monica (an informant) goes on to explain that girls who are considered unattractive have to perform more sex acts for drugs. "Those with desirable attributes, or with connections to crack dealers, have great control over their lives" (Williams, 1992, p. 113). There are still women who perform sex acts for drugs, but women who have looks, connections or money can make their own choices (Williams, 1992).

Carl Taylor (1993) interviewed female gang members on the issue of carrying a weapon. Why are females carrying weapons?

Pamela, 24:

Call it violence if you want, but I say it's just taking care of yourself. If everybody else is packing, you be dumb as fuck to not have some kinda protection. When all the gangsters, rapists, killers, crazy babes, boys, and little kids wouldn't have their heaters maybe that's when I'll stop having my gun, that ain't violence, that's just straight and staying alive (p. 100).

Kiki, 20:

You need a gun `cause it's lots of ignorant assholes out in the street. Men think `cause you little, or a woman, they can do whatever pleases them. Girl, you know it's always some tramp ass bitch or some gangster niggah talking trash and girl, y'all know you got to be ready for anything (p. 102).

Delores, 24:

> Girls got guns for the same reason guys got `em, it's wild out here, you need to protect yourself. Street law is the same, tough and it regulates itself. You have to regulate niggahs, especially if you're in the business. It don't matter if it's selling crack, weed, or any kinda dope, business is business. Guns protect you and your business, right? (pp. 102-103).

Taylor (1993) interviews several gang members about their attitudes toward females running neighborhood drug businesses. He interviews Pat, 24, who heads her own corporate crew with five female employees and three males. The interviewing team saw Pat arrive in her Black Volvo 740, and a `vette pulled in behind her. In the `vette was Robert, one of her male employees. The appeared to be arguing. When the interviewer asked Pat what the argument was about, Pat responded:

> It's just ho shit, crying `bout monay, typical shit from boys who think they can run things better. Rob always crying `bout girls can't do shit. He's a little crybaby ho. I am in business, making monay is hard these days. If I listen to people illing all the time I couldn't make monay or do anything. Oh, it's like crazy some days, but they make more monay with me then with their old crew. Rob is mad `cause it was his cousin and brothers who got popped and went to Jacktown [Jackson Prison]. When I took over, this here clique was making ho paper. Why, `cause Rob and his boy Ralph was hitting the pipe, and letting every little skeezer in the `hood get credit or just giving freebies away. I had worked in this thing since I was fifteen. I was in school working twelve hours everyday. My people didn't know I was working one of the big houses for the X organization. That was like school, they taught me how to cook the shit.
>
> When I was sixteen, by boyfriend started to move up in the X. I just

learned more things, this was my education. This is a career. Why
go to college for a career? I go to community college to learn other
shit, but this here is my livelihood. My boyfriend got shot when I
was eighteen. It was fucked up, his own boys set him up and fucked
him up, he was lucky, `cause all he wanted was to kill his boys after
that hit. I had other things to do, and you know people who will kill
for monay, so just get them and forget all that other shit. At twenty
I bought my own car; now before, I had got a car from my man, that
was sweet, but then he would always talk `bout he bought this and he
did this, fuck being the little toy ho, buying your own shit is much
better.

Me and this big fella started to kick when I was twenty-two, he had
the juice, big juice. I met all the real players with this fella, it was
sweet. Plus, I was getting it on, `cause my man let me get some of
his products directly from his source. Soon, I was cruising and had
my own serious crew. When I got my first car it was on, like dick
and balls, ha ha ha ha, whoa! My next car was real def; you see, this
muthafucka was real shitty when I bought my first car. My brothers
and some of his friends cut the deal with the sales guy. He thought
he was some smooth dressing pretty boy, but he's a ho, ha ha ha ha,
anyway he dissed me like I was skeezing or some little ho that was
getting her first car from a man. So next time I took the girls, and we
talked shit, and dogged his silly ass. When he saw my monay, I
thought he was going to piss on himself. Ever since that he knows I
am Ms. Pat, and he gives me much play. Still I drive a little car at
work, and we don't drive our fly shit all over the hood. See, I am
running a enterprise, okay? This is serious shit and I'm going to make
all the dope monay I can; why not, it's `bout time girls get some
monay that's real and not for sacking. (pp. 117-118)

Vicky:

It's simple, girls is gangsters just like fellahs, we can do anything the
fellah can do, and anybody that think we can't is ignorant and dumb.
Ain't no man gonna rock us, we rule our own shit, this is our own
thang, only bitches that is getting dogged is the ones that let it
happen. We ain't letting it happen to us. This crew is small, but we

getting it on, we getting it on! (p. 119)

Pat:

The hardest thing for some fellahs is taking orders from a babe. Now
Rob is mad `cause I am doing the shit they should have done. But,
these fellahs is carrying their dicks in their hands all the time. Rob is
mad when I gets paid, mad `cause I won't buy no little 190 Mercedes
like those tramp ho's that live off their dope men. Me, it's my thang,
no one is in charge but me. I'm not buying no little dope ho car, not
the kid, I'm a business woman, and everybody going to respect me.
I keep my monay, not some shit talking lawyer, it's my thang and you
got to understand that I will kill to keep my shit from falling, got it?
Okay? Rob and his boys better get to it or they can get the fuck out
of Dodge, I'm nobodies ho! There's fellahs who know what time it is,
and they making bank. The silly boys talk `bout bitches, and they got
no bank. (p. 119)

Taylor (1993) was not the only researcher to include interviews with female
gang members in his book. Elliott Currie (1989), in his book *Dope and Trouble*, also
included interviews with female gang members. Currie's interviews also illustrate
the independence and aggressiveness of female gang members. He interviewed
Tasha, a Black female, on the subject of how she started selling drugs for herself.

One time I started trying to teach my friend how to sell drugs. At this
time, I had stopped selling for anybody. At this time, I had stopped
selling for anybody, I was just selling for me, I had that much money.
So me and my friend, I was trying to show her. (p. 76)

It was like I was making, say, I think it was a lot of money to be so
young. I was making like a thousand dollars every two days.
Because I didn't sell like little rocks, I sold big rocks. I'm talking
about this much of a rock was like five hundred dollars. And I'd sell
this to the big dope dealers so they could break it down into a lot to

make his money, to make a whole bunch of money. (p. 80)

Unlike White females, many Black females have always had to be independent, strong, and economic supporters of their family. It is possible that the structural position and the behavioral alternatives resulting from that has contributed to the nature of African-American female gangs. It appears that today, African-American gangs run by females have become as violent, aggressive and profit oriented as their male counterparts.

Early gang research efforts had their flaws in charting the historical emergence of female gangs. This is because most early research projects neglected the roles of female gang members. I will specifically address the issues facing female gang members.

Because Black females, and the Black community in general, have suffered the most during periods of economic recessions/depressions, it is important to study the effects of generations of dependence on welfare, and lack of support from absent fathers continue to impact the conditions of women. Is the continuous chain of poverty an incentive for young Black females to join gangs and start their own crews?

In summary, this research will contribute to the literature on these issues in a variety of ways. First, there is very little literature on Black female gang members; what literature exist on gangs has conflicting messages about the role of women in gangs. It is important to clarify what is taking place among African-American female gang members. Secondly, gang members are an integral part of the social and economic system we live in and we are indisputably uninformed on how these women construct their lives. Third, we need to establish a scientific base of literature that examines the Black female underclass's relationship to the informal economy and what their relationships are to males in their communities. And finally, the literature that focuses on the interrelationship between race, class and gender rarely focus specifically on Black underclass women.

CHAPTER VIII

Anomie: Women, Inequality and Innovation

According to Merton, 1938, "frustration and thwarted aspiration lead to the search for avenues of escape from a culturally induced intolerable situation" (p. 689).

Merton's theoretical perspective stems from the tradition of Emile Durkheim's nineteenth century writings on anomie and normlessness (Pfohl, 1994). According to Durkheim, anomie is the result of rapid social change which leads to social disorganization and normlessness. Durkheim was concerned with massive social change which was occurring in France at the time he was writing. He watched French societal arrangements move from a pre-industrialized, less complex social structure where everyone worked together as a social unit (this type of social arrangement he titled mechanically organized), to a very industrialized, complex, individualized social structure (this type of society he labeled organically organized). Anomie describes the state of normalessness that Durkheim theorized societies experienced during this transformation. "Anomie was a discrete problem, a historically specific problem of societies in transition from traditional to the modern world" (Pfohl, 1994, p. 253). Durkheim felt that anomie was a temporal dislocation which emerged during rapid social change and a transition from a traditional society to a more modern society. During this transition humans are no longer directed by a shared moral code, but by an insatiable greed. "Durkheim suggested that anomie unleashed an instinctually based form of human greed, the pursuit of unlimited aspirations" (Pfohl, 1994, p. 253).

Merton's extension of the anomie perspective grew out of the influence of Durkheim's interpretation of European society during the late 19th and early 20th century. As it was for Durkhiem, unlimited aspirations and greed were major concerns for Merton. Merton's theory stressed the importance of aspirations without clearly defined limits and unequal access to culturally valued material rewards. Merton's theory focused on the relationship between culturally valued goals and the access to the legitimate means for achieving those goals. Merton hypothesized that people in American society share a common desire to achieve the "American dream"- material wealth. However, Merton believed that not everyone could achieve these culturally induced goals. Not everyone has access to legitimate means to achieve the goals prescribed as obtainable by society. Therefore, Merton theorized that individuals would adapt in one of five ways to the strain of the discrepancy between the expected goals and differential access to legitimate means to achieve those goals (see Table 1).

"Merton's analysis of deviance reveals a set of adaptations to the socially structured contradiction between goals and available means of goal attainment. Each adaptation contrasts with the path of conformity" (Pfohl, 1994, p. 263). Conformists are those who accepts both the socially prescribed goals and uses legitimate means to achieve those goals. They have no reason to deviate from culturally defined goals and means. They have the right family background, quality education, and follow cultural prescribed rules.

TABLE 1

Merton's Typology of Individual Adaptations to Anomie

	Cultural Goals	**Availability of legitimate means of goal attainment**
I. Conformity	+	+
II. Innovation	+	-
III. Ritualism	-	+
IV. Retreatism	-	-
V. Rebel	+	+
	-	-

Source: Robert K. Merton (1957) *Social Theory and Social Structure*. Glencoe, Ill.: The Free Press.

They go to school, they work hard, get promotions, and in return reap the material benefits which are afforded to them by following these rules. In contrast, innovators are those who desire the culturally prescribed goals of material wealth, but don't have, or don't use, socially defined legitimate means to achieve those goals. They want the material rewards society dangles in their face, but are unable to attain them legitimately. Cultural norms prescribe certain definitions of success which includes accumulation of material wealth, however, not everyone has access to legitimate means to achieve this goal. Therefore, they used non-sanctioned and sometimes illegitimate means to realize the "American dream." They discover that they are getting nowhere by following the rules. This is the group that chooses to deviate and enter the informal economy to fulfill their dreams.

Let's think about the African-American women discussed in the literature review. This is clearly a group that has been denied access to legitimate means to achieve their goals of material wealth. Therefore, it would be naive of us to think that those so deprived would not abandon legitimate means and find new avenues to reach socially sanctioned goals. They realize that a minimum wage job is never going to afford them those things that define success in American society. Some African-American women may resolve this conflict between culturally prescribed goals and socially prescribed means by obtaining valued material wealth through illegitimate means. Innovators emerge in a society that sets up highly valued goals without giving equal access to the legitimate means to all members of society. We live in a society that puts a lot of emphasis on affluence but does not provide equal access to structurally approved means for realizing those goals. The innovator finds creative, illegitimate ways of realizing their dream. In the setting of this research, the illegitimate means is the sale of illegal drugs. Many of the women interviewed in Taylor's book (1993) alluded to this very concept. They talked about making money, buying fine cars, and the inability to have these without selling drugs.

The ritualist does not desire the culturally prescribed goals of society but accepts the socially desired means of achieving those goals. They do not care about being at the top in business, or owning all the fine material items society says you need to own to be successful, nor do they really care about playing by the rules. This person just puts in their time and goes home, caring very little about owning material indicators of success. Ritualists desire only to get through the day and settles for the basics in life. However, they will go to work without making waves and they will not enter the informal economy to reach an unattainable and undesired goal.

The retreatist on the other hand rejects both the culturally defined goals of society as well as the socially defined means of achieving those goals. According to

Merton (1938), they have given up on normal societal aspirations and the desired means of achievement. This person has given up on conventional life. S/he drops our of the race for desired societal means and goals. Their form of adaptation is to escape typically through the use of drug or alcohol. This is the group that constitutes the customer base for drug dealers. Cloward and Ohlin (1960) believed this group to be double failures. They suggested that this group failed in both the informal and the formal economy. They had no choice but to drop out, give up.

The rebels constitute the final group of deviants that Merton describes. The rebels reject both the cultural goals of society as well as the social means of achieving those goals, but is different from the retreatist in that the rebel sets up his/her own goals and means. This group makes up their own cultural standards of success while defining their own unique means of achieving those standards. The rebel replaces "dominant goals and means with something better" (Pfohl, 1994, p. 265). Pfohl (1994) maintains that, like the other forms of adaptation the rebel is a normal outgrowth of the contradictions in a stratified society.

Cloward and Ohlin (1960), add a missing element to Merton's theory. They discuss the unequal access to illegitimate opportunities as well. They theorized that not only are legitimate opportunities unequally distributed, but so are illegitimate opportunities. Therefore, those who are involved in the illegitimate activity of selling drugs are there because the opportunity is available to them. They live in the right neighborhoods which give them the opportunity to enter the informal economy at this level. Therefore, the strain from discrepancies between goals and means not only compels people to construct deviant alternatives, but the environment also determines what deviant alternatives are available. For example, the bank teller would have access to and knowledge of embezzlement opportunities whereas the ghetto dweller would have access to and knowledge of drug dealing. The environment and your location in the economic system and employmement sector determines your access to illegitimate opportunities as well as legitimate.

In addition to the strain between the discrepancies in goal attainment and means, Merton also made reference to the structured inequality that made the strain toward anomie more pronounced; and, when a society or community is in an anomic state, social norms and social control mechanism lose their power; they lose their ability to control.

According to Messner and Rosenfeld (1994),

> Merton implied that this anomic quality of life is responsible for the
> high rates of crime and deviance characteristic of the United
> States. He also proposed that similar socio-cultural processes account
> for the social distribution of crime. The pressures toward anomie,
> according to Merton, are socially structured. They became
> progressively more intense at lower levels of the social class
> hierarchy, because obstacles to the use of the legitimate means for
> success are greater in the lower classes. (p. 12)

One of the critiques of Merton's (1938) work which is congruent with this research is it's focus only on the lack of equal opportunity. Merton believed that by giving equal access to everyone to attain their dreams, their dream could eventually be realized. What he neglected was to recognize that the political and economic structure of capitalism itself was what was prohibiting equal access to political and economic resources. Therefore, according to Gouldner (1970), partial reforms within the current system are not enough; capitalism must be replaced with democratic socialism. An economic system which would not only allow equal access to wage labor, but access to the means of production and the distribution of the material benefits of those productions. Even if wages are increased and there is greater access to employment opportunities workers "will still be denied access to the means by which economic activities and economic payoffs are socially structured" (Pfohl, 1994, p. 288). Those who control the means of production will continue to benefit from the labor of those workers they exploit. He goes on to state,

> . . . as such, unequal access to culturally desired goals and high rates of deviance will continue as well. Efforts to structurally reduce the systematic character of anomic deviance must go beyond the liberal orientation of the perspective as traditionally formulated. (p. 288).

Regardless of the limitations of Merton's theoretical approach, and the critical theory caveats of it, the theory remains the most obvious explanation of the type of deviance this research project explored. The female gang members referenced in the literature review are denotative of what Merton (1938) labelled the innovator. Excerpts from Taylor's (1993) book will assist in strengthening this conclusion. The chapter on the economic conditions of females should negate any debate about the restricted access to equal opportunities experienced by this particular group. So I would like to focus strictly on the females responses to their limited access.

In Chapter V, The History of Female Gang Involvement, there are several quotes from Taylor's books (1990, 1993) that make reference to the frustration that emerges from the discrepancy between the goals and means among the women he interviewed. For example, Lynn talks about making paper (money), having nice clothes, and fine cars. Harriet talks about how her crew is not on welfare and how she sees benzo's, beemers and jeeps right in the city. The girls are making money just like the fellahs. And Vellicia concludes that "everything is `bout monay" (Taylor 1993, p. 97).

Some responses from males interviewed in Taylor's (1990) book illustrate that their perception of the lack of opportunities (legitimate means) to make money. Rafael answers the following question: what are your chances of taking up a legal job or getting into a program that will train you for a better job? Rafael answered:

> Better paying jobs ain't in this world for bloods, especially young bloods. I been kicking it with a crew since I was thirteen. I ain't telling y'all where but I got my paper stashed and I'm still rolling. Some of the fellahs after that got busted, had to join job training fake-ass programs. Train you for what? A cook? Bullshit janitor job? A security guard that pays $3.65 and hour? Or maybe one of those good paying skilled jobs like welding. Year, welding, that's what my brother did at Dodge Main until they laid him off, after fourteen and a half years they said, we'll retrain you." Right! Yo, he already has a skill! They gave my brother some paper for his time and told him to go to the re-training center. he went and some preppy bitch dissed him, the bitch acted like she was better than him. Made him feel real bad, made him feel like he was begging, groveling for her black ass working for the lying-ass whites. I told him fuck that perpetrating fake-ass bitch. So he took his money and got with me and the crew and now he's rolling. We got some straight legal shit. Can't tell y'all `cause the hook always trying to dog. (p. 57)

Dickie on the subject of working:

> Work in a plant? Plants be noisy, and have mugs screaming bullshit orders—and they pay ho-wages. That money ain't shit compared to rolling. I'm going to roll until I leave here. My momma talks about how proud she is of me making doughski. She used to say I wasn't shit, but now she's proud. See, when you getting paid, everybody, I mean everybody, want to get with you. (p. 55)

Carl Taylor (1990, 1993), never specifically inquires about the discrepancies between goals and means among his female interviewee's but he does ask them about making money. Most agreed that they get involved in selling drugs for the money. But is this the result of limited access to the legitimate economy. I will consider this relationship in my findings chapter. I expressly address this question in my survey instrument. I will ask the respondents if they see alternatives to welfare and drug selling in their community. If they respond negatively, saying there are no alternatives, then I can speculate that these women are cognizant of the discrepancies between goals and means which I attribute to the inherent contradictions of a capitalist economy. I will examine the data for some indication that these women agree that using deviant alternatives to get money is acceptable in their community (whether the deviance involves selling drugs or collecting welfare). It has already been made apparent in Taylor's (1993) research that women join gangs and sell drugs for the money, his research can be expanded by asking: are there legitimate alternatives to obtaining wealth within your community? If so, what are these alternatives?

CHAPTER IX

Research Questions

In the spirit of grounded theory and some postmodern considerations, traditional, dichotomous breaks between theory and methods ought not be maintained. Accordingly, though the following research questions arise from the nature of the problem and the theory used to interpret and explain it, the methodological requirements for its examination also flow from these considerations. In the following section I treat the research questions and the required analytical methods to examine the data as a single statement of approach.

1.   Do African-American Women live at income levels below those of white women in society? Secondly, does this have any effect on their involvement in gang or informal economic activities? Many researchers have noted and reported on the economic conditions of African-American women (Huff, 1990; Leiman, 1993; Malveaux, 1985; Simms, 1985; Sowell, 1984; Sparr, 1984). According to Leiman (1993), race remains the single most powerful predictor of poverty among women. And when factoring in the increasing rates of out-of-wedlock births among black teenagers, more than one-half of all children born to Black female-headed households

live below the poverty level (Huff, 1990). As noted earlier, according to the 1991 census data, 26% of all Black families live below the poverty level, while only 7% of White families do (see Table 2).

TABLE 2

Incomes Below Poverty Level: Poverty Index Statistics

	ALL	WHITES	BLACKS
Percent of all persons designed poverty status:			
NATIONAL STATISTICS	13.0	10.0	30.0
INDIANA	10.7	10.0	29.1
FORT WAYNE	7.6	9.0	33.3
SOUTH CENTRAL FORT WAYNE	39.8	13.9	39.5
Families below poverty:			
NATIONAL STATISTICS	10.0	7.0	26.0
INDIANA	7.9	7.0	26.3
FORT WAYNE	5.3	7.0	31.7
SOUTH CENTRAL FORT WAYNE	27.3	11.5	39.5
Female headed households, No husband, with children Under 18 years of age:			
NATIONAL STATISTICS	44.0	35.0	77.0
INDIANA	47.2	47.7	72.5
FORT WAYNE	57.4	57.0	84.2
SOUTH CENTRAL FORT WAYNE	48.2	28.4	54.2
Males 15 years and older percent employed full-time, Year round:			
NATIONAL STATISTICS	53.0	54.2	44.9
INDIANA	54.5	55.5	42.1
FORT WAYNE	53.6	55.8	41.1
SOUTH CENTRAL FORT WAYNE	53.0	54.0	44.9

Table 2, Con't.

	ALL	WHITES	BLACKS
Females 15 Years and Older Percent employed Full-time, Year round:			
NATIONAL STATISTICS	33.9	33.6	35.0
INDIANA	33.4	33.4	33.5
FORT WAYNE	36.2	35.7	38.7
SOUTH CENTRAL FORT WAYNE	33.9	33.6	35.1

Source: United States Census Data. (1991).

For Female headed households, with children under 18 years of age the percent of those living below the poverty level gets even higher, for Black female-headed households 66% live below the poverty level, and for white female-headed households the percent living below poverty is 35% (see Table 2). In Indiana the figures are 47.7% and 72.5% respectively. Women in Indiana tend to be worse off than the National average. The first part of the question, as illustrated above has been answered by the literature as well as in the tables drawn from the 1991 census data.

Through combining face-to-face interviews with census data, I will construct the economic conditions of Black women at the site of my research. What is the percentage of Black women living below the poverty level? Do these women consciously perceive their level of relative deprivation? And, finally, I need to determine if the percent living below the poverty level is higher in South Central Fort Wayne than national and local statistics. If women from this area report high levels of gang involvement and high rates of women selling drugs in their community, then maybe we can further substantiate that economic conditions can lead to involvement in illegal drug sales and other gang related activities. Joining the informal economy may be one way of adapting to their perception of relative deprivation. Some literature supports this economic theoretical approach to crime (Beirne & Messerschmidt, 1991; Messner & Rosenfeld, 1994; Weisheit, 1990).

I will attempt to determine if the interviewees perceive an increase in female gang members; and if there are families selling drugs; and whether females are making money just like the male gang members. I will also be sensitive to the extent to which respondents perceive the problem of economics and joblessness as the reason why some females are turning to gangs and selling drugs to make a living.

Responses should include statements of activities which are convergent with what is known about the informal economic activities of male gang members. Do these female gang members compare themselves and their understanding of the informal economy to the activities and understandings of their male counterparts? Statements should also include implicit or explicit indicators of change in their behavior or in the behaviors of others like them in their informal economic activities which correspond to the males informal activities.

2.   Do African-American women involved in gang activities in lower class communities view themselves and other Black women in their community as violent and aggressive as their male counterparts?

Since the emergence of corporate gangs, few researchers have dedicated their research to understanding the roles of female gang members (Anderson, 1992; Huff, 1990; Lyman, 1989; Taylor, 1990). Those who have studied female gang members, have focused their attention on Hispanic women (Campbell, 1984; Harris, 1988, Horowitz, 1984; Quicker, 1983). However, Taylor (1990) specifically interviewed female gang members and asked them why they were joining gangs. And even more recently, Taylor devoted an entire volume to the activities of female gang members (1993). Taylor (1990) found that women involved in drug trafficking crews are more specialized and violent than ever before. Several women in Taylor's book (1993) when asked about violence responded that "you got to be violent to take care of business, and you got to pack a weapon to protect yourself from the streets" (p. 67). Others talked about how they do the same things as male gang members, including using violence to protect themselves and their business interest (Taylor, 1993).

Since there has been an emergence of corporate gangs in Fort Wayne (the site of my research), I would expect to find the same attitudes towards violence that Carl Taylor (1990, 1993) found in his research project. That is, a pattern of responses indicating that females involved in gangs, selling illegal drugs, or both are just as sure about the use of violence as those females that Taylor interviewed. However, given the size of Fort Wayne, there might not be as much violent activity among female gang members as Taylor's (1993) research might have suggested.

In order to examine this research question, I will look specifically at statements about violence or aggression in the responses of my interviewees. These statements may be made about themselves or others like them. I will look at verbal references to the number of violent acts between women that they have been eyewitness to. I will also look for statements by the interviewee that refer to violence or aggression they have used; references to uses of violence by other female gang members, or by their peers who are not necessarily involved in gangs. And finally, references to any justifications for the use of violence or aggression by themselves, female gang members, peers, etc.

3.   What are African-American female gang members in lower-class neighborhoods views toward the economy?

Since the abolition of slavery, African-American women have had to take low paying, dead-end, degrading jobs, while being left alone by Black males to raise and support their families (Leiman, 1993). According to Simms (1985), the Black female-headed household has the highest poverty rates among all families in the United States, with the exception of Hispanic female-headed families, as mentioned and supported in the literature review.

I will attempt to determine if these negative attitudes exist among African-American females: negative attitudes toward the job market and negative attitudes about current economic conditions among women like them (Black and living in lower-class communities). Taylor (1990, 1993) and Jankowski's (1991) respondent's consistently referred to the poor economic conditions in their communities and lack of legitimate employment. Jankowski (1991) even pointed out the entrepreneurial spirit of many gang members. One quote from a young man interviewed in Jankowski's article stated "Ethics don't pay the bills, money pays the bill, and I'm hustling to get money" (Jankowski, 1991, pp. 102-103). Lynn who was interviewed in Taylor's book reported that the girls in the crew got paper just like the fellas. And Tasha, from Elliott Currie's book *Dope and Trouble*, reported making about a thousand dollars every two days. All three research projects also noted that these women knew that this was the only way to make lots of money, and that these women were aware of their impoverished economic conditions, and that it was much easier to make money illegitimately, than going legitimate (Currie, 1989; Jankowski, 1991; Taylor, 1990, 1993). I will search for this same sense of lack of opportunity in the legitimate job market and this same perception that the only way to make real money is through joining a gang and selling drugs. If the women I interview are also aware of the economic conditions and lack of job opportunities in their community, they should have a negative attitude toward the legitimate economy, while recognizing that some women need to participate in the illegal economy to support themselves and their families.

I will be sensitive to what the interviewees say about their job histories, availability of jobs, and any abstract representations of discrimination. I will also explore their attitudes toward the future and what it looks like for them and their peers. How do these women cope with comparisons of their economic conditions and employment opportunities with both Black and White males and White females? Do these frustrations contribute to their involvement in gangs and informal economic activities?

4. What are African-American female gang members in lower class communities views toward racism?

As early as 1851, as made evident in Sojourner Truth's statement at the women's rights conference, Black women have been aware that their experiences are different from those of Whites in general and more specifically White females (hooks, 1981). Women of color in the poems compiled in *This Bridge Called My Back* describe how radically different they are from not only White women, but Black men as well. Many of the books and articles by Black women and me have noted how the imperialist, white supremacist mentality, and male superiority has left Black women in a unique position politically and economically; and, noted that this view of society is what has left women of color at the bottom of the social class hierarchy (Cooper, 1892/1988; Davis, 1944/1981; hooks, 1981; Leiman 1993; Wallace, 1990; Wilson, 1987).

The question that has not been specifically addressed by previous gang literature (Anderson, 1990; Williams, 1993) is whether or not female gang members feel that American society in general is racist. In what follows I will look for patterns that illustrate the frustration that was expressed by feminist scholars who have discussed their feelings of oppression in their works (Cooper, 1992/1988; Davis, 1944/1988; hooks, 1981; Wallace, 1990). All these Black feminists theorists revealed how their feelings and experiences were quite different from those of White women.

In my findings chapter, I will note exemplars which may reveal similar levels of discomfort among interviewees: How do they express their frustration and discomfort with being a Black female in a White, male dominated society? I will also be looking for abstract analyses of racial and sexual discrimination. Are there illustrations used to indicate that Blacks get treated differently than whites? Males differently than females? And finally, I will encourage the respondents to share any implicit or explicit examples of racism or discrimination they or their peers have experienced.

5.   Do African-American female gang members in lower-class communities view gang and/or society as sexist?

Rice (1963) found that, in New York, both Black and White female gang members could do nothing to gain the same level of respect as male gang members. Bowker, Gross and Klien (1980), found that female gang members were excluded from the activities viewed as significant in their gangs, such as planning and carrying out certain crimes. More recently, however, Taylor's research in Detroit indicated that along with the increase in all-female gangs, and the increase in the use of violence and aggression among females, perhaps the female gang members are taking on a more significant, possibly more equal, role with their male counterparts (Taylor, 1993).

The economic condition of the inner-city Black female may be fostering the emergence of a more violent aggressive female, that sees selling drugs as an alternative means to attaining their goals. Historically, African-American females have been the sole providers and protectors of their households (Davis, 1944/1981; hooks, 1981; Wallace, 1990). Using this cultural context, it may be that Black women in gangs will take on a more powerful role in those communities as well.

Although the literature does not directly deal with whether female gang members feel the oppression of sexism, I am predicting that they do. Especially, given the history of Black females and the fact that their role has been so different from the roles of Black women in gangs as reflected in the literature. It is almost as if African-American females in gangs have taken on the stereotypical white female role (passive and submissive) which contradicts much of the literature on the African-American woman.

But Taylor's research (1993) suggests that females in gangs are becoming more independent. Hence, as researchers we should look for some kind of feminist movement within gangs that may parallel that of the formal economy.

In order to support this argument, respondent's involved in gangs, and in lower class communities in general, would need to express their concerns about the way female gang members are being treated consistently, and express opinions that would lead the interviewer to believe that they know the men are not treating them as equals, and they are doing something about it. I have also designed a question to look at whether or not African-American females feel the pressures of sexism from the larger society. I asked further if they felt that they are treated differently, by society because they are a Black female, and if so how are they treated differently, and is that different from the way white females are treated? Also, are there expressions of change occurring over time in society or within gangs between males and females? And finally, I will be looking for any indicators of abstract conceptions or analysis of sexism within society or within gangs.

CHAPTER X

Methods and Epistemology

The methodological approach that I have chosen for this research project I have entitled feminist standpoint ethnography. The reason I have chose the feminist standpoint epistemology is because the traditional feminist methodological approaches have had several problems. The major critique of traditional feminism is that of its emphasis on gender essentialism. One of the consequences of gender essentialism—including placing all women in one category, more specifically, considering all women as white women—has resulted in yet another form of ignoring or silencing the Black female. It assumes that Black women are like white women but because of their race, they are even more exploited and oppressed. According to Harris (1990),

> as in the dominant discourse, Black women re relegated to the margins, ignored or extolled as just like us, only more so. But Black women are not White women of color. Moreover, feminist essentialism represents not just an insult to Black women, but a broken promise—the promise to listen to women's stories, the promise of feminist method. (p. 248)

It is important that we as sociologists, both male and female, move away from this gender essentialist approach to understanding the experiences of women of color and move toward understanding women of color based on their own views of their sociological and political aggravations, expressed in their own language (Collins, 1990; Rollins, 1985; Sudarkasa, 1986; Warren, 1988).

Efforts to avoid gender essentialism is only one step in producing qualitative research that improves our knowledge base of African-American experiences. We must also move away from the social scientific assumption that people of color have no differential identities. "in fact, the reproduction of a singular monolithic identity as objectified reality is a must if people of color are to remain oppressed" (Stanfield II, 1993, p. 21). To acknowledge the differences in identities among people of color would actually threaten the dominant political, social and economic arrangements (Stanfield II, 1993). Perhaps this is why Martin Luther King, Jr., during the 1950s and 1960s, tried to get through to the public that all Blacks were not one dimensional and passive as portrayed in the media and in some social science research efforts (Stanfield II, 1993).

Ellison (1964) argued that researchers cannot reduce the richness of African-American experiences to statistical tables. Standpoint feminist theorist have also noted the oppressive nature of objective knowledge in understanding African-American cultural diversity. In their classical research efforts, these feminists have noted how the male-centric epistemologies, paradigms, theories and methods have contributed not only to the contents of our research, but more importantly to the conduct of our research. The male-centric approaches to understanding phenomena has used its power to create, interpret and disseminate knowledge (Abramowitz, 1982; Bernick, 1991; Christman, 1988; Currie, 1988; DeVault, 1990; Grant & Ward, 1987; Lother, 1986; Marburg, 1981; Mascia-Lees, McKeganey and Bloor, 1991;

Peplau & Conrad, 1989; Rapp, 1988; Sprague & Zimmerman, 1989; Warren, 1988; Williams, 1987, 1990).

According to Denzin and Lincoln (1994), it is very difficult to document and study the cultural relevance of African-American experiences while embracing the White male-centric epistemologies dominant within the social sciences.

> This resulted in Afrocentrists' contradicting themselves by claiming to be producing knowledge sensitive to the experiences of African-descent peoples as a unique cultural population even as they insist on using Eurocentric logic of inquiry that reduce the knowable to the measurable or to evolutionary or linear variables. (p. 182).

Oppressed peoples, especially women of color, have few opportunities to express the way they construct the realities of their lives. Allowing them a voice and an opportunity to share their experiences would give them some form of empowerment (Denzin & Lincoln, 1994). As long as we use traditional forms of research methods to understand a culturally unique group of people, the experiences of women in lower-class communities will continue to be silenced. We as a society will never understand how these women construct their reality based on race, class and gender.

"Critical ethnography is a type of reflection that examines culture, knowledge and action. It expands our horizons for choice and widens our experimental capacity to see, hear, and feel:" (Thomas, 1993, p. 2). African-American women's experiences in conventional theoretical and methodological research approaches have been ignored and omitted in social science literature. Even though their lives can provide a rich fabric of social life, especially with regard to race, class, and gender. Margaret Andersen's research suggest that conventional eqistemologies are counter to that which requires white scholars to produce a more inclusive and less distorted account of race, class and gender relations (Andersoen, 1993). We, as social scientists, can not continue to make value judgements and assessments based on traditional research approaches that clearly function to repress the cultural richness of the particular group of women that I have chosen to study, namely lower-class African-American females.

CHAPTER XI

METHODS: LOGISTICS

I have conducted my research in South Central Fort Wayne, Indiana, which was, for me, the largest and most convenient accessible city. I attempted to identify potential interviewees through networking with Black and Hispanic social service professionals in the Fort Wayne area. My father is a Methodist minister in the community, and he was able to put me in contact with Black ministers who were working with gang members. I also acquired access to interviewees through networking with initial respondents. Some of the respondents agreed to give me names of other women whom they knew would agree to an interview.

Respondents who were interviewed took part in a face-to-face, semi-structured, tape recorded, interview. I had designed specific topic areas that emerged from the literature, but I gave myself and the interviewees enough freedom to discuss other topics which emerged from the original questions (see appendix A for questionnaire and Appendix C for complete transcribed interviews). I asked the respondents indirect questions about drug and gang activities in their communities. Even though they felt open enough to share their own experiences, I assured them that I would not disclose any information given to me about any specific details or behaviors of the interviewees. An effort was made to keep their responses as unattributable as possible. In this I honored the agreement with the Human Subjects Review Board at Western Michigan University.

The questionnaire was designed to obtain information about the nature and content of female interaction in underclass, urban communities, as well as, their attitudes and opinions on important issues (i.e., racism, sexism, violence, drug dealing, the police and education). Questions were designed to get at the following information: are Black women in inner-city, underclass communities generally as aggressive as their male counterparts? Are these women involved in gang activities like their male counterparts: aggressive, violent and dealing drugs? And, finally, do these women express their feelings of resentment towards racism, sexism and classism in their community as well as in society?

The sample came from several different neighborhoods in what is referred to as South Central Fort Wayne. The area runs east and west on Oxford street from Anthony to Hanna and North to Toledo Street. My sample consisted of nine African-American Females and one racially mixed female (Black father and White mother). Of the ten respondents, seven were admittedly active in gangs at one point in their lives. Three respondents had not been involved in gangs, but were familiar with what occurs in the community where gangs were active. I included these three interviews because there were very few young women I could locate in Fort Wayne who would admit to being involved in gang activity.

Contacting the Sample

I had contacted the Mayor's office, the police department, the Director of Public Safety, the Fort Wayne Urban League, and many other organizations, but received no responses. Therefore, to get more subjects the only remaining option I had was to hang out on the street corners where known gang members also congregate. This did not seem like the safest option for me given my size, skin color and gender.

Of the three interviewees who were not gang members, two of them were in Narcotics Anonymous. They had never been in a gang, but had contact with gang members when they were buying drugs. One respondent was neither a user, nor a gang member. I made contact with her through Job Works--an employment agency. Because I was having difficulty making contact with gang members, I agreed to interview the two women from N.A. and the one female whose only criterion for inclusion was that she lived in South Central Fort Wayne. I felt that her view of the community may be an interesting addition to the views of females who are, or who have been gang members, as well as, those who have been on the other side of the drug selling, gang activities as buyers.

All but three of the respondents had completed high school and the age range for respondents was from 21 to 33 years of age. Three of the respondents had children and none of the respondents were married. Eight of the respondents came from single parent homes. Two of the eight were raised by their fathers and one was raised by her mother until she was fifteen, and then she moved in with her father. That was the extent of the personal, demographic questions that I asked. The survey instrument was designed to avoid personal questions and was confined to inquiries about the level of violence and gang activity in the community in general.

I had originally planned to interview between 15 and 20 females who had been, or were still active in gangs. However, once I began to collect my data, as aforementioned, I realized how difficult it was going to be to get interviews with young women from the underclass who admittedly had been or are involved in gangs. Although my sample was smaller than I had originally intended, I felt that the completed interviews would be sufficient for several different reasons. First, of the ten interviewees, seven were known gang members, or at one point had identified themselves with a gang. Secondly, three of the respondents had a relationship to the community I was studying, and could be used to make comparisons with, or corroborate the stories of the gang members. Thirdly, I felt that the respondents were very open, honest and articulate in their responses. These were quality interviews which can contribute to the current literature and be used as a basis for developing approaches for securing the desired larger sample.

Initially, I had planned to make contacts with Black professionals in the community who were working with gang members through their churches, or through gang task forces. I did get a few interviews through ministers in Fort Wayne, one through a teen center in Fort Wayne, one through a Job Works program, other contacts were made through an introduction of a Narcotics Anonymous member to whom I was introduced by an administrator at Job Works. And, finally, I obtained several interviews through gang members themselves who gave me names of other contacts.

As indicated above, I had originally planned to interview 15 to 20 women who, at one point, had been in a gang. However, I experienced great difficulty and encountered many barriers when trying to collect my data. I naively thought that the Black professionals in the community would be willing to work with me in establishing interviews. While most seemed willing, they never contacted me with any names. Several even stated that they didn't trust what I am doing and questioned my reasons for desiring to speak to the informants. I am not real sure if the difficulty came from being white, very petite in stature, being an academic, or being female or a combination of all four. I felt as if the Black male professionals thought that what I was doing was an undergraduate, insignificant project; while the Black female professionals expressed their discomfort with my being White and wanting to make contacts with Black females. Along the way, I had even volunteered my time to help out in anyway I could with their programs. I volunteered to serve on the drug/gang task force, volunteered to help out at the urban League, Women's Bureau, etc. I received no acceptance of any of these offers, nor did any of these groups help me to make contacts with African-American females that I could interview. I eventually became very dependent on a Hispanic male who introduced me to some of his contacts who directed me to women who agreed to complete the interviews. I think one of the major problems was my student status; also, I am not from Fort Wayne, nor am I known in the Fort Wayne community. Finally, I had identified myself with Western Michigan University, another unknown entity. Therefore, there was no reason for these professionals to trust that I was interested in, and wanted to do something that may help their community.

I must admit it was very difficult as well as intriguing crossing race and class lines. But, once I made contact with the interviewees, I was very surprised by their openness and the graciousness with which they greeted me. Overall, I am convinced that the sincerity of these women's stories emanated not only from their dignity and honor, but also from my willingness to express how I felt, to deconstruct the role of the researcher, and share my experiences based on race and class.

CHAPTER XII

Findings

Several research questions emerged from the literature review, I will examine them individually, then consider the issues that emerged serendipitously out of the responses which were not directly related to the research questions.

The Economic Conditions of the Sample

The first research question addressed the level of economic deprivation among African-American females in under class communities. I chose the communities in South Central Fort Wayne for my research, because it is known as one of the poorest areas in Fort Wayne and a known underclass Black Ghetto. If I were to understand the respondents feelings of economic deprivation, and the relationship that this might have to the involvement in the informal economy (i.e., selling drugs), it is important that I chose an area of Fort Wayne which was defined as poor to conduct the research.

Increased labor force participation has not translated into economic stability for women. Today women raising families are the fastest growing group joining the poverty ranks. These single mothers are often sole providers for their families. Although many of these women are entitled to child support, most men are delinquent in making such payments. These women have inadequate resources to provide child care or to provide basic needs for themselves. Most of these women living in poverty, while raising their children, also work. However, women, especially minority women, have been restricted to jobs with low-pay and limited potential for advancement. The single female who heads the household is also discriminated against for training and employment opportunities, which also constitutes an enormous impediment to financial security (United States Commission on Civil Rights, 1983). Margaret Simms (1985) also alluded to the increasing poverty rates of women and children who are members of single parent households. National and local census data also support these previous accounts (See Table 2).

As the local statistics indicate, although over one-half of all Black female single-headed households report income levels below poverty, the area I choose to study is doing much better than the national average, Indiana in general, as well as Fort Wayne. Although the percentage of all people in this community living below the poverty level tends to be higher than local, state and national statistics (See Table 3), the percentage of African-American females who are single-parents living below the poverty level tends to be much lower in South Central Fort Wayne than that of the City of Fort Wayne, as well as Indiana and the National statistics. However, if Black females work full-year, full-time, as reported in the local and state and national statistics, the percent below poverty level is very similar. Therefore, I feel I made an appropriate choice in studying this particular community. Although Black, female, single parents are faring better than national, state and local women in similar positions, the community as a whole tends to be reflective of these statistics. Therefore, relative deprivation may be a very salient issue within the area I have defined in South Central Fort Wayne.

Table 3

Median Family Incomes: National, State and Local Income Levels

	ALL	WHITE	BLACKS
Median Family Incomes			
NATIONAL STATISTICS	30,056	39,613	23,161
INDIANA	34,082	34,897	22,359
FORT WAYNE	31,981	33,460	22,866
SOUTH CENTRAL FORT WAYNE	17,635	23,625	16,853
Males, age 15 and over			
year around, full-time:			
NATIONAL STATISTICS	29,237	31,487	22,191
INDIANA	28,197	28,427	24,946
FORT WAYNE	25,990	26,431	21,950
SOUTH CENTRAL FORT WAYNE	18,494		
Females, age 15 and over			
year around, full-time:			
NATIONAL STATISTICS	19,570	20,904	18,702
INDIANA	17,101	17,103	17,161
FORT WAYNE	17,585	17,808	16,899
SOUTH CENTRAL FORT WAYNE	15,000		
Married couple			
households with children			
Under 18 years of age:			
NATIONAL STATISTICS	40,693	44,606	36,479
INDIANA	39,285	39,404	37,692
FORT WAYNE	42,671	37,788	37,608
SOUTH CENTRAL FORT WAYNE	29,467	33,601	26,878

Table 3 (cont'd)

	ALL	WHITES	BLACKS
Female headed households			
No husband, with children			
Under 18 years of age:			
NATIONAL STATISTICS	12,485	15,662	9,705
INDIANA	12,789	14,184	8,708
FORT WAYNE	16,060	16,077	11,630
SOUTH CENTRAL FORT WAYNE	12,147	14,760	11,567

Source: United States Census Data. (1991)

It is also important to look at the types of positions held by each category in the table. When the respondents talked about jobs, they mentioned the type of work that they would be able to get, and most of them referred to low-paying, service jobs. Is that the reality for African-Americans in the area defined as South Central Fort Wayne? As you can see in Table 4, African-Americans have the highest percentage of workers in the service industry and administrative and clerical support positions. It is even higher in Fort Wayne and South Central than the state and national average. Nearly, 37% of all Blacks in South Central fit into one of these two occupational categories (See Table 4).

In sum, South Central Fort Wayne's levels of poverty are similar to national, state and local averages, as are the types of positions held by race, class and gender reflective of the larger social structure.

Gender and Gang Structure

Before asking the interviewees whether or not they felt that African-American females in their neighborhoods joined gangs because of economic deprivation, I had to ask them how many females were in gangs, and if they felt there were any all female run gangs in Fort Wayne. This was asked to determine if women were starting to break away from male gangs as was reported about Detroit in Taylor's books (1900, 1993). All of the respondents said that there were no all female gangs, but females were running with male gang members. The reports of no all female gangs changed the nature of my study. I could not investigate the attitudes, beliefs and actions of females who are in gender mixed gangs. Previous literature (Taylor, 1993) had reported all female gangs. However, this appears not to be the case in South Central Fort Wayne. Females are still operating with and within male structured gangs.

Table 4

Percent in Occupation by Race: Employment by Race and Gender

	WHITES	BLACK
Executive:		
NATIONAL STATISTICS	13.1	7.6
INDIANA	10.5	6.9
FORT WAYNE	11.6	6.2
SOUTH CENTRAL FORT WAYNE	7.3	3.9
Professional:		
NATIONAL STATISTICS	14.7	10.4
INDIANA	12.1	9.5
FORT WAYNE	13.3	7.6
SOUTH CENTRAL FORT WAYNE	6.3	7.5
Technicians and related support:		
NATIONAL STATISTICS	7.2	8.3
INDIANA	2.0	1.4
FORT WAYNE	2.4	1.3
SOUTH CENTRAL FORT WAYNE	2.1	3.1
Sales:		
NATIONAL STATISTICS	12.4	7.6
INDIANA	15.4	8.0
FORT WAYNE	13.0	6.6
SOUTH CENTRAL FORT WAYNE	7.3	7.2
Administrative Support and Clerical:		
NATIONAL STATISTICS	16.2	18.4
INDIANA	15.1	18.3
FORT WAYNE	17.7	14.1
SOUTH CENTRAL FORT WAYNE	16.5	13.1

	WHITES	BLACK
Private Household:		
NATIONAL STATISTI CS	0.3	1.2
INDIANA	0.2	0.6
FORT WAYNE	0.3	0.4
SOUTH CENTRAL FORT WAYNE	.6	.8
Protective Service:		
NATIONAL STATISTICS	1.6	2.7
INDIANA	1.2	2.4
FORT WAYNE	0.9	1.2
SOUTH CENTRAL FORT WAYNE	2.7	1.0
Service Occupation:		
NATIONAL STATISTICS	9.8	18.2
INDIANA	10.9	20.1
FORT WAYNE	11.3	22.7
SOUTH CENTRAL FORT WAYNE	10.4	26.2
Farming, Forestry and Fishing:		
NATIONAL STATISTICS	2.4	1.4
INDIANA	1.9	0.4
FORT WAYNE	0.6	0.3
SOUTH CENTRAL FORT WAYNE	2.9	.2
Precision Production, Crafts and Machine Repairs:		
NATIONAL STATISTICS	11.7	8.1
INDIANA	13.2	16.5
FORT WAYNE	11.2	8.7
SOUTH CENTRAL FORT WAYNE	9.6	8.5
Machine Operators:		
NATIONAL STATISTICS	3.9	6.3
INDIANA	9.3	6.9
FORT WAYNE	10.2	20.5
SOUTH CENTRAL FORT WAYNE	19.4	16.0

	WHITE	BLACK
Transportation and Material Moving::		
NATIONAL STATISTICS	3.1	4.3
INDIANA	3.6	3.2
FORT WAYNE	3.5	2.8
SOUTH CENTRAL FORT WAYNE	4.9	4.1
Handlers, Equipment Dealers, Helpers, Laborers:		
NATIONAL STATISTICS	3.6	5.5
INDIANA	4.6	5.8
FORT WAYNE	4.0	7.6
SOUTH CENTRAL FORT WAYNE	10.0	8.4
TOTAL		
NATIONAL STATISTICS	100	100
INDIANA	100	100
FORT WAYNE	100	100
SOUTH CENTRAL FORT WAYNE	100	100

Source: United States Census Data. (1991)

Red Dog:

No all female gangs males and females run together. Both males and females sell drugs. Whoever want to do it can. How much you make depends on who you sell to. But I think females are makin' as much money as males. Most ain't usin' drugs, they just trying to make a living.

Sandra:

There are a lot of female gang members, but no all female gangs. They are doin' the same thing as male gang members. If they want to sell drugs, they sell drugs. I think women are better at sellin' drugs, because most people trust them to be honest, just like the guys, some girls makes lots of money, but most just gettin' by. The sell what they have to make ends meet.

The other eight respondents answered this question in the same way. Which leads me to conclude that there are no female gangs. It is important to note that there may be several reasons why I did not find all female gangs in South Central Fort Wayne. First, drug selling gangs are a relatively new phenomenon in the Fort Wayne area, as they are in many other medium size and smaller cities. It is possible that autonomous female gangs have not emerged because of the brevity of the existence of gangs in this area. In most large cities (Chicago, Detroit, Las Angeles, New York, etc.) recorded histories of gang activity can be dated back almost 100 years. And current literature adequately documents womens involvement in male gangs prior to their existence as an independent group (Campbell, 1984; Huff, 1990; Quicker, 1983; Taylor, 1990, 1993). The finding of no all female gangs may be the result of this short history of gang activity in the Fort Wayne area. Secondly, this finding may be the result of the absence of a critical mass. My experience with my sample impressed upon me the lack of density of gang members in Fort Wayne. It is possible that there are not enough women involved in gangs in South Central Fort Wayne to start and support their own gang. Finding no all-female gangs changed the nature of my research and will be discussed in the conclusion chapter of this document.

Reasons for Gang Membership

When asked why females are involved in gangs, most (9 out of 10) responded that it was the money. Most agreed that you can't find a decent job, especially if you don't have beyond a high school education.

Red Dog:

`cause they ain't givin' nobody out here no jobs. You'll try for couple of months, but ain't no one goin' call you back. Then when you get a job they get snotty with ya' and try to fire ya'. You can make more money on the streets selling drugs. Ain't nobody goin' put up with that stuff for the pay they try to give ya'.

Sandra:

They ain't no jobs out here. No one goin' hire someone like me. I ain't never had a job, and ain't no one goin' to give me a chance. Most people around here have to collect welfare or sell drugs, or both. Sometimes when I go in to apply for a job, the manager won't even give me an application `cause he says I ain't qualified. He don't know shit about my qualifications. I think a lot of young people are forced to sell drugs `cause there ain't no jobs around here. You certainly can't go to the north side of town and look for a job. They be asking you what your black ass is doin' on that side of town. Every time I go to the north side the police stop me `cause they know I don't belong here. Than when you do get a job the bosses always suspicious thinking you goin' steal something from him, or give something away to your friends. I hate that. They pay you bullshit money, then they constantly harassing ya'.

Tenise:

There ain't no jobs for people like me. I don't have enough education or experience to get nothing but a minimum wage job. That's bullshit workin' for minimum wage. It ain't worth it. That's why these cats are out there sellin' drugs. They got to give people like us good paying jobs, or at least a chance to prove we can work hard. Most the time you get hired they already assume you lazy and ain't going to work. I don't like working for minimum wage when they treat you like a criminal. No one has to put up with that. I'd rather collect welfare or sell drugs. At least when you sellin' you're your own boss.

Shelia:

People get involved in selling for the money, attention, to fit in with the older guys. This is the same for female sellers. Actually, the guys prefer female gang members. They don't mess up the money, and when someone don't want to pay them they don't back down. Most are selling crack cocaine 'cause that is where you make the most money. You can find crack on any corner. You have to ask who sellin' marijuana, but both males and females can be found selling crack on any street corner in this area.

Temika:

Most people get involved in selling, because it is the only way to make money around here. It is hard to get a job that pays more than sellin'. Most people don't think sellin' crack makes you money, but they're a lot of young people around here who are living on their own and takin' care of their mothers only because of selling crack. They couldn't make that kind of money workin' no minimum wage job. Most people like me can't even get a minimum wage job. They laugh you right out of their business when you ask for an application. It's sad that you can make more money selling drugs, but that's the way it is.

Dieonne:

Yeah! for one thing I can say it's for the money. For example, my mother was a drug dealer and she did it for the money. She got high off of makin' the money. There ain't no jobs out there for women and people you would call disabled. I am not justifying people sellin', but that's just the way it is.

All of the respondents, with exception of Theresa, echoed the same response Theresa felt that women got involved in selling drugs, because they didn't know better. Theresa, however, is a college student, who had never been in a gang. Her mother taught her the value of an education, and she feels that this is the route that young Black women should take to be successful.

Most of the respondents reported that they could not find employment, and that women are involved in gangs for the same reason males are, to make money.

They realize, just like their other male counterparts, that the informal economy can be much more profitable then a low-paying clerical, or service job, which most claimed to be qualified for. Some of the respondents reported that it is difficult for them to even get a low-paying job. They see themselves as being no different from male gang members who are selling drugs. They understand that selling drugs is one of the few ways to make a living, given their race and educational levels. I will deal more extensively with the race issue later.

Females and Violence

This research question deals with the issue of violence used by females in drug selling cultures. If females are involved in selling drugs, are they as tough and aggressive as the males in that part of the informal economy? I asked two different questions about this issue. First, I asked about females carrying weapons and second about fights among females. When respondents were asked about violence and its relationship to selling drugs, all of the gang members agreed that if a person is selling drugs, they must be willing to use violence. If you are selling drugs, male or female, you have to use some form of force to protect yourself and your property.

Red Dog:

Anyone who sells drugs has to be violent, even if they female. It is part of doin' business.

Sandra:

I guess females would have to be as violent if they sold drugs. I saw this sick sister kick this dudes ass 'cause he owed her some money. If a bitch is really into dealing, she'll carry a gun and ain't afraid to use it just like the guys.

Tenise:

If you sellin', you've got to be violent. A lot peoples take advantage of ya' if you ain't willin' to use force. Someone think you weak, they goin' take from ya'. Even if you female you got to be willin' to shoot.

Shelia:

Yes, women are as violent as men. They fight each other, they fight guys, sell drugs, wear colors, they do everything the guys do.

Temika:

Female gang members do everything the guys do. They beat each other up, they fight over drugs, they carry guns, sell drugs.

Denise:

Females fight alongside males. You've got to be just as violent as males. Females who are soft won't make it.

Debra:

There are not a lot of females sellin', but the ones who are, are just as violent and mean, and make just as much money as men.

Most of the respondents agreed that females who sold drugs had to be as aggressive and violent as the males in the drug business. The respondents who did not believe that women are as violent as men, were the same respondents who did not report ever being involved in gang activity. It appears that the respondents who have actually been in gangs, or are still in gangs, reported that violence is necessary when selling drugs, and that females who are in the business have to be as violent as their male counterparts. The justification for the violence was to protect yourself, your business and your reputation as a dealer. You can't be seen as soft when you're dealing.

Perception of Economy

This topic deals with the attitudes of these women toward the economy. In order to see how they felt about the job market and the economy in general. I asked them two questions. The first was about their neighborhood and their personal attitudes toward welfare. The second question dealt with their opinions on what types of job opportunities are available within their community. All ten respondent's felt that welfare was necessary, and did not blame the mothers who were on welfare. Most agreed that a women has to do what she can to feed her family.

Red Dog:

Yes, no one dogs anyone for tryin' to feed their kids. Most people can't find no jobs, the babies have to eat. Everyone knows this.

Denise:

Most women in this area are collecting welfare and sellin' dope out of their houses. It is kind of dangerous when you got kids, so some they just live off their welfare checks. I don't know of any jobs around here for women where they can make as much money as they do sellin' crack. I think a lot of women be smart when they collect welfare `cause they get all the benefits. Most women who work don't get any health insurance for their kids, so they just never take their kids to the doctor. If the kid gets sick they end up sellin' a little on the side anyways to pay doctor bills. Most women in this neighborhood get welfare `cause they care about feedin' and takin' care of their kids. That's the only way to do it. Ain't nobody going to hire us for much more than minimum wage, and if they do they say it's part time work ya' forty hours a week, and don't give you any health care plan. Also, it cost a lot of money to have someone watch your kids while you're at work. If you're dealin' or on welfare, the kids can stay with you.

Debra:

Yeah. Most people think welfare is O.K. Nobody's going to criticize someone for gettin' money and food stamps so that they can feed their kids. It's hard to find a job out there where they offer you any kind of money. Then when you do work you get treated like dirt. These people hire us for minimum wage and then think they can treat us like slaves. We're still human beings. Welfare, or sellin' drugs allows you to keep your self respect. People around here respect women for doin' what they can to feed their babies. Especially when everyone seems to be against them. White employers.

These findings are consistent with the responses to the first research question. If these respondents feel that there are no opportunities for good paying legitimate jobs, then they will also agree that welfare is something that is seen as necessary and important. Most of the respondents reported that women on welfare are doing what they have to in order to feed their children. As the literature indicates (Currie, 1989; Jankowski, 1991; Lawson, 1992; Leiman, 1993; Simms, 1985), the employment opportunities for Black, female, single-parents, are not very good. This is made evident in the 1991 census data as well as in the works of Huff (1990), Leiman (1993), Malveaux (1985), Sparr (1984) and Simms (1985) who reported on the economic conditions of African-American women. Currie (1989), Jankowski (1991) and Taylor (1990, 1993) specifically address the relationship between economic deprivation and entry into the informal economy.

In an effort to clarify the answer I asked the women if they see any legitimate alternative to welfare for women in their community. If they are cognizant of their economic conditions, and limited employment opportunities, then I assumed that most would respond to this question negatively, reporting that there really aren't too many options for making money, outside of the informal economy and welfare.

Nine out of the ten women interviewed felt that there were no alternatives to welfare for single parents. The one respondent who said that there were opportunities was never a gang member, but a recovering drug addict who shared her own experiences and talked about how she had gone to school to be a court reporter and that many women in the area could do the same, go to school and get a job.

The following quotes are the responses to the question about alternatives sources of income, outside of welfare.

Red Dog:

A lot of women are on welfare and sellin' drugs. Neither one pays high enough so they got to do both. Most women around here don't like to leave their children and go to work. They can't find work anyway.

Sandra:

No one can find a job in this neighborhood, especially if you got kids. You can't afford to pay someone to watch them. Most women collect welfare and sell drugs for their men.

Shelia:

Most people get welfare 'cause there is no alternative. They get money the best way they know how.

Kaye:

[Alternatives] for females, prostitution, strong armed robberies, conning. People in my neighborhood are always lookin' for a victim. If you want to work, for example, I had no skills or nothin', but when I got clean and wanted to work, there was plenty of jobs, there are plenty of jobs, like restaurants, janitorial, McDonalds, if you want to work.

Those respondents who reported that there was work, like Kaye, indicated that the jobs that were available were in the service industry, low paying, dead end positions. Denise, also referred to this type of occupation as the major option for work available in her community.

Denise:

No. Well maybe, if you wanted to take a low paying job that you can't get anywhere with. Anyone can get a job. But who wants to hire someone like me to do a job that has some responsibility, and pays well? I was in charge of at least ten brothers and sisters runnin' drugs. I had to take care of the money and weigh the dope. I can handle a little responsibility. In the real world you can't get no respect.

From the responses that I received, it is very evident that they know that there are not many employment opportunities available for them. The women who mentioned legitimate alternatives gave examples of employment such as restaurant work, janitorial work, cooking, etc., all of the stereotypical underemployed positions. Several of them even mentioned that many women are not only collecting welfare, but they are also selling drugs for additional money. If there are no high paying, respectable jobs in a community for African-American women, where do we expect them to work? If they are working, how do we expect them to pay child care and health insurance? The jobs that are available for this population are jobs that don't typically offer health care benefits, nor do they provide child care. The lack of alternatives to welfare reflect the consequences of continuing racism and discrimination. However, the respondents in this community, don't blame any woman for doing what she has to, to feed her children.

The existing literature (Davis, 1944/1981); hooks, 1981; Leiman, 1993; Wallace, 1990; Wilson, 1987), strongly supports the fact that institutionalized racism and sexism have a great deal to do with the economic conditions of women in urban communities and American society in general. I wanted to see if these women were actually aware of the degree of racism within their communities as well as within society as a whole. For analytical purposes I will confine the discussion to racism, although many interviewees responses allude to both racism and sexism within their detailed descriptions of color based discrimination. Sexism will be dealt with when discussing the final research question.

Perceptions of Racism

None of the previous gang research has specifically asked the gang members if they think society is racist, but many of the respondents come across as being overtly angry at a racist system (Taylor, 1990, 1993). I asked my respondents directly if they felt society was racist. I will also return to some of the discussions about employment opportunities where the responses covertly reveal subtle forms of racism.

When I asked the respondents if they thought society was racist, and if they thought White females get treated differently than Black females, nine of the ten respondents felt that society was racist, but most did not agree overtly that White females were treated any differently than Black females. However, the responses do manifest illustrations and examples which indicate that they do see some subtle differences in the way White women are treated by Black men and by employers. One respondent talked about how there are more White women working than Black women, so maybe they are treated differently. While others talked about how Black men treat White women as if they are special or Prima-donnas.

Some of the responses on the racism issue clearly show that these women feel the intensity of a racist society, and understand the dynamics of racism in America. Whether they understand completely how racism affects them is still questionable, but the women I interviewed were very cognizant of, and able to articulate, their feelings of concern about racism in our society. I believed that this group had to be aware of overt and covert racism, primarily, because of their social class condition. This is the group that bears the brunt of a racist society.

When the respondent's were asked about society being racist, I received the following responses.

Red Dog:

> Yeah, especially on the job. When you workin', they always watch you when your friends come in. They think you're going to give your friends something extra. Think you're gonna' give away free food to your friends. Also, I can't walk down Coldwater [road in the predominately white north side of town], the police will stop me, ask me what I'm doin' and take me to jail. One time I was in a store and a county cop followed me all over the store. They think most Black people always out stealing. You can't ever go to shows 'cause white people always look at ya' funny. I don't think they treat white people this way, especially white females.

Sandra:

> Yeah. I think people are racist, because they always stop and look at me funny, and think I'm going to rob them or beat them up. Everyone is sacred of you if you black. It is funny sometimes, but other times it hurts. I feel like people think Black females are all mean and loud. They look at us funny when we hang together trying to have a good time. If we get real loud they get all shitty. If there are a bunch of young White girls in the mall, gettin' loud, everyone thinks they cute, or ignores them. In that way I thing Black girls get treated differently. I don't mean to offend you, but if you got loud, and was having fun, nobody would probably say nothing.

Tenise:

> I think we get treated a little bit differently than White females. But I don't know, 'cause I don't know how you get treated. But it's like

every time I go to the store with my friends the managers, or security, are always following us around. Like they think `cause we Black we couldn't afford to buy nothin' so we must be stealing. They always think Black people are going to steal something. I think Black girls have lower self-esteem `cause they always treated like they're poor or on welfare. In that way I think they are treated differently than White girls.

Shelia:

Yeah. I think society is racist. For example, they kicked this Black kid out of school, because he was defending himself from a White guy. They never even asked the Black guy his side of the story, or checked out the White guy's story with the other kids, they just kicked him out, `cause he was Black, it must have been his fault.

Kaye:

Yeah, `cause in my neighborhood, which is predominately black, if a white person comes in, it's like what's this mother fucker want, yeah we goin' get him, or automatically think he's a sucker, and he goin' get beat. Yeah, like I'm on both sides of it. I go to my moms and it's niggah this and niggah that, and on my dads side it's honky this and honky that, and I'm just like where do I fit in? I had an identity crisis for a long time. The children, in my opinion, of White families show less respect for parents, and in the Black family, even though they get less [material things], they respect their parents. They see that the parents do what they can. Even though it's just a little they respect their parents for what they give them. When a White girl comes into the neighborhood, even if she with a Black guy, she gets treated like a primadonna, she gets more attention, and the Black girl basically has lower self-esteem `cause of the way she treated. In the neighborhood where I live, there're some White girls usin', but because they white, no one thinks they're usin', but if they in that neighborhood everybody's usin'.

Debra:

Maybe, it seems like everybody always plays Black folks as stupid or uneducated. I know lots of Black people who are goin' to college, or have good jobs. Not all Black men are sellin' drugs. That's what most people think, that the Blacks are sellin' the drugs. Blacks might be sellin' drugs, but we ain't the ones bringing it into the neighborhood. I don't think there's much difference between black and white females. Maybe white females, sometimes get treated like they're queens or something. Nothing personal, but a lot of times when brothers see a White woman, they talk like she's something special. But I don't think they respect her.

Many of the respondents referred to the low self-esteem among Black females which may also ensue from institutionalized racism and sexism in our society, as previously alluded to in the literature (Cooper, 1892/1988; Davis 1944/1981; hooks, 1981; Wallace, 1990). Also, in the questions dealing with job opportunities, many respondents talked about employers not hiring people like me or us. The respondents were referring to their race, economic status and gender. It appears from the preceding literature and the responses that I received, that Black women are aware of and sensitive to the oppression of racism. As discussed earlier, due to the nature of the research, I can't make generalizations to the entire Black female population, nor was that my initial intention, but theses responses can make a contribution to the self reported incidents of oppression by published Black feminist scholars (Cooper 1892/1988; Davis 1944/1981; hooks, 1981; Wallace, 1990). However, most of these aforementioned researchers view their oppression as a combination of living in a patriachical and racist society. The oppression is a combination of race, class and gender, with race being the most salient element to this triumvirate of casual factors.

Perceptions of Sexism

This brings me to the final research question which pertained to the levels of sexism experienced by this group of respondents. As discussed previously and supported by the literature (Davis, 1944/1981; hooks, 1981; Wallace, 1990), African-American females have assumed the burden of being the providers and protectors of the Black community. However, given the unique conditions of a patriarchical society, they have been pushed to the bottom of the socio-economic ladder (Leiman, 1991). Political and economic histories outline the oppression and disadvantages faced by African-American women within the existing political and economic system (Leiman, 1993). This has often left African-American women single and responsible for not only young Black females, but Black male children as well. However, patriarchy has limited their ability to act out these roles that were required of them prior to the abolition of slavery (Leiman, 1993). Also some contemporary literature on female gang members indicates that female gang members are appendages, or sexual objects of male gang members (Bowker, Gross & Klien, 1980; Rice, 1993). While Taylor's (1993) research demonstrates that the levels of aggression and independence among Black female gang members is increasing which appears to be a more accurate portrayal of the level of independence and strength that has always been characteristic of African-American women as demonstrated in the Black feminist literature (hooks, 1981; Wallace, 1990). I also inquired about the strength and independence of the women in the community I researched. Again, I was conducting the research under the assumption that Black females would be developing their own gangs as a symbol of the independence and strength as mentioned earlier (see conclusion for further discussion). Because of this, I felt that it is even more important to look at how these women respond to, their attitudes toward, and their feelings about patriarchy in their community. Do they feel that they are different than males, and if so, why? If they reported different treatment of females why?

Because respect is a big question in this community and in many communities like it, I felt that the best approach to understanding their feelings toward sexism is by asking the respondents if they felt that women god the same respect as men in society as a whole and within gangs. I would also like to return to some other questions, not specifically on sexism, but questions in which these women's answers very specifically allude to much covert and overt sexism.

The first question I asked was whether or not women got the same respect as men in or outside their neighborhood. Three of the ten respondents answered yes, that women do get treated with respect. However, two of the respondents who answered yes put a qualifier on their answers. For example:

Tenise:

If you treat guys with respect, they'll respect you. A lot of girls get dogged 'cause they do stupid shit. But most of the time the girls get treated the same as guys.

Debra:

Yeah. I think girls get lots of respect. The only girls not respected around here are the ones that are givin' it up for drugs, or are sellin' themselves to buy. Most women get respect if they sellin' drugs, but not if they using. It's ok for guys to use, but not us.

The third respondent who said that women get the same amount of respect as men didn't expand on her answer. She just said "yes" with no further explanation. Most of the respondents who answered "no" to this question responded in ways similar to the answers to the question about female drug dealers getting respect; where the women mentioned that they have to earn respect. Many of them talked about earning respect by being tough, not selling yourself, and not being soft. Women could earn the respect of their male counterparts, the community and society by being just as tough, mean, and aggressive as males. They have to earn respect in ways that exceed the standards for their male counterparts. These are the same qualities that women must adopt in order to succeed in the formal economy. However, Black women taking on these qualities within the formal economy are seen as too aggressive and threatening to the male structure, but it appears that these qualities are necessary, and contributes to success in business and respect from peers in an underclass community, whether operating legitimately are not. Maybe Miller's (1958) focal concerns (smartness, toughness, excitement, trouble and fate) could apply to females from lower-class communities as well as males.

Here are some of the negative responses I received when asking about females and respect.

Red Dog:

Younger girls gettin' treated wrong, many messing around having babies and ending up on welfare. But if you treat men with respect, they treat you with respect. Sometimes people in this area act like men know everything, but things are changing. Women are gettin' more respect.

Sandra:

I think it is harder for girls to earn respect than guys. Guys just beat someone up, or carry a gun and they get respect. But girls, if they mess up, they get treated like a ho. You get to watch who you sell to and hang out with when you're a girl, 'cause the guys will mark you as a ho and an easy fuck, and they'll try to take advantage of you. But as you get older you learn how to take care of men, and they start treating you better.

Shelia:

Guys get more attention, and women do not get the same amount of

respect on jobs. Males have better opportunities. The bosses think
`cause they guys they will do a better job. For example, I was job
hunting with my boyfriend and they said they would hire me if they
hired my boyfriend. Then when they hired us, they said they hired
my boyfriend and I at the same time so he could train me. I had a
high school diploma and he didn't, but they thought he would catch
on quicker and be able to train me. When my boyfriend got fired,
they never put me back on the schedule.

Temika:

Yeah. I think girls get treated differently. I don't think they get as
good of jobs. Most employers will hire guys first, `cause they think
they'll do a better job. Guys around here don't respect women much
I think it is because of all the rap music bashin' women. I listen to
some of this music calling women bitches and ho's and it upsets me.
I think the guys around here think sex is all we're good for. They'll
use us when they want some, but they don't really give a shit about
what happens to us after that.

Thersa:

No, they don't get the same respect. If a man does something, he
thinks it is done right. If a woman does something, the man thinks he
has to follow after her so it is done right, but the truth is, if a woman
does it, it will probably be done right. Yes, society is prejudice
against Black women, the media makes her out to be someone that
don't do nothing. All society do is put them down. This lowers
Black women's self-esteem.

Kaye:

Definitely not! because if a girl, I got more respect by sellin' myself
than if I did by just havin' a boyfriend outside the G's, but if a guy
give it away it's alright, but if a girl gives it away she is labeled as a
slut or a ho. Now there's a difference between a whore and a slut. A
ho get the money and a whore gives it away. And a woman gets
more respect if she chargin' and not just givin' it. If a woman shows
she deserves respect, she ain't goin' to get it without a fight, but she
will get it.

Denise:

I think women get respect if they earn it. Women who prostitute
themselves, or have sex for drugs don't get any respect. But if you
work, sell drugs, or get welfare to take care of your kids you get
respect. I think girls have to work harder to get respect, but when
they prove their tough, they get it. In gangs, women who get beat in
get more respect than those who have sex. Like if you a girl and you
enter the gang the same way men do, by gettin' beat up, you're a full
member of that gang, just like the guys, but if you have sex with the
gang members to join the gang, they'll always treat you with
disrespect. Like you a ho or something. You'll never get rid of that
title.

As with racism, this particular group of females realizes that they are treated

differently based on gender. Many stated that they can eventually get the same

amount of respect as men, providing they work hard and earn it. I internalized the

level of frustration about the different treatment when personally talking to these

women. For example, Shelia appeared very agitated by the fact that her boyfriend,

who didn't even have a high school diploma, was suppose to train her for a job. And

Theresa appeared very upset when talking about how society sees Black women as

doing nothing which lowers the Black females self-esteem. Similar responses were

elicited when I asked them about respect given to female drug dealers. Again, most

felt that respect could be earned, but only if you did it the way the guys did. Women

had to be tough, aggressive and not allow anyone to take advantage of them. It was

also made evident by the responses that women had to, again, work harder to earn

this respect. However, most felt that this respect could eventually be earned.

Red Dog:

If you have respect for others you get respect in return. I think some women get more respect, `cause they are women who are tough as hell, and they are also women who don't take no shit off anybody.

Tenise:

If they're makin' good money they get lots of respect. Just like the guys, if they make good money, they earn respect.

Denise even talked about the parallel between women in the informal economy and those in the legitimate business world. She talked about how women have to take on certain characteristics in both economies in order to earn respect. Although most Black feminist literature critique the White feminist descriptions of masculinity in our society, the women from this particular community seem to talk about the reality of those masculine qualities, and the need to adopt those qualities to survive.

Denise:

Yeah. Most women if they actin' like men get the same respect as men. Those women who act aggressive and will do anything to get to the top, get to the top, and get respect. Those who sleep their way to the top, or are too soft ain't goin' to get the same respect.

Many of the respondents actually made reference to those stereotypical White feminine qualities as being a determining factor in the responses of others in their culture. By acting traditionally female, you actually lose respect. Therefore, not only are Black females from this particular lower class community familiar with the stereotypical female qualities, but recognize that these qualities can hold women back, not only in the illegitimate economy, but in the legitimate business world as well.

Serendipity and Future Research

There are some issues that were not specifically addressed by the research questions, but did suggest interesting directions for future research. They are more attitudinal responses to questions. More specifically, respondents attitudes toward the police and the educational system. What are African-American female gang members in inner-city, lower-class communities views toward the police? Joan stated that the police are clearly the enemy when being interviewed for Terry Williams book, *Crackhouse* (1992). Many cops try to patrol the neighborhoods, but because of the sheer numbers of buyers and sellers, it is impossible for the police to do anything about it. Most people in the community feel that the police are corrupt anyway (Williams, 1992). Headache (a male respondent in Williams' text, 1992) says

> the police really are the enemy. They don't seem to want to fraternize, even though they are not death on the crack scene, as I expected they would be. It's more like they keep a distance, just sort of watch us, watch the scene. That's what I see (p. 86).

He goes on to discuss how, unless there is a shooting, that the police only continue to watch from a distance, but if someone who is not a local enters the neighborhood, they will hassle them (Williams, 1992).

This current move toward the hard line, drug policy has made many inner-city youth and adults aware of the focus on their communities as the country's leaders belabor the need to fight crime. Increases in police officers and dollars given to these communities to fight crime, make the police very visible in these communities. However, the youth involved in selling drugs do not respect or fear the police. They have already rejected every other conventional institution in society, why would we expect them to accept what the police are doing as legitimate? They have rejected education, and most have moved away from their families. All that can be accomplished by increasing patrol cars is to make people within these communities very resistant to the extra enforcement and very angry about the policies' interference within their neighborhoods. William (1992) goes on to say.

> that criminal justice bureaucracies have obtained substantial increases in funding each year, both in actual dollar terms and as a share of the total government budgets. This has limited or prevented increases for education, welfare, employment, and social services—efforts that could help alleviate the economic and social inequalities that many inner-city residents endure. In effect, anti-drug policies have taken inner-city residents' attempts to do good and transformed them into institutionalized racism. (p. 89)

James Baldwin (1962), a Black novelist and commentator on racism wrote about policing inner city neighborhoods:

> Their very presence is an insult, and it would be, even if they spent their entire day feeding gum drops to children. They represent the force of the white world, and that world's criminal profit and case, to keep the black man corralled up here, in his place. The Badge, the gun holster, and the swinging of the club make it vivid what will happen should his rebellion become overt. (p. 66)

I expected to hear indications of negative attitudes toward the police, whether implicit or explicit as well as similar thoughts regarding their perceptions of what the police are doing in their neighborhoods. Are they there to protect the people in the community? Or, are they there to harass Black people? I would expect that most people, based on what the literature has expressed, will assume the police are in their neighborhoods just looking for and often causing trouble. I expect to find that the women interviewed will feel that the police are racist, and that the police believe drugs are being sold in every Black, lower-class community.

I anticipated statements about police honesty, police brutality, police effectiveness and police mindlessness. Other patterns that I expected to find recurrent among respondents are statements about opposition of police to the respondents illegal activities, personal experiences with the police as well as positive or negative attitudes toward the police. As you will see in the following responses, this is exactly what I found—negative attitudes toward the police.

All of the respondents agreed that most people in their neighborhood think that the police are not there to help. Most qualified their responses by saying, that if they know you they'll help, or when you are using or dealing you don't think they are there to help, but once you sober up, go straight, you realize they are. But the majority of Blacks in South Central, according to my respondents, feel that the police are only there to harass. This response tends to be consistent with the literature (Baldwin, 1962; Currie, 1989; Taylor 1990, 1993; Williams, 1992).

Following are some of the responses to the question: would most of your friends agree that the police are there to help? Why? Why not?

Red Dog:

Police, if you know them they will help, but if you don't they won't help. Most people around here disrespect the police. Most of the time the police just look and harass. They ain't here to help.

Sandra:

The police aren't here to help us. They are here to protect the white folks from us. Most of the time if we call the police, they ain't goin' to show.

Tenise:

Most people would say the police aren't here to help. It's just like the teachers they get paid whether they help us or not.

Shelia:

Most people hate the police, police are only here to hassle. They see them as trying to stop them from what they think is right (sellin'). Selling is right for them, and the police are just in the way of business.

Temika:

Police don't help shit around here. They won't even come into our neighborhood unless they driving around real slow staring at us, as if we were freaks. Most people don't like the police. Cops don't get no respect.

Kaye:

If you're usin' or sellin' they're harassing. They are there to F with you, but if you're just a residential person tryin' to make ends meet, then they're there to help.

Dieonne:

Yeah. Today I do, when I was doin', no. Users they think the police is a bunch of bullshit. I thought they just wanted to be there to try and arrest me and others, and I didn't think they were there to help the community.

As supported by the literature, through the works of Currie (1989), Taylor (1990, 1993) and Williams (1992), and this research, there is clearly disrespect and distrust of police officers. I think Baldwin (1962) was right when he said that having the police patrolling these areas is insulting, if not a blatant form of racism. Not because they patrol their area, but because of the way they patrol their area. Proactive policing focuses on Black lower-class communities which increases arrest rates among Blacks reinforces racial stereotypes while contributing to the hatred and distrust of police officers by Blacks in lower-class neighborhoods (Samaha, 1994).

To examine the issue of racism and policing, I asked the respondents if they and/or their friends refer to the police as racist. Eight out of ten respondents said that the police are racists. The other two respondents, both gang members, said that they didn't know, but gave examples of police behavior that, on the surface, seems overtly racist. In order to determine if the polices' behavior was racist on the basis of these examples, I had to ask myself, would the police respond the same way to a group of Whites, or in a all White neighborhood? In most cases the answer was no.

Denise and Debra, the two that did not come right out and say police are racists, had this to say about the police:

Denise:

You mean racist as in treat Blacks differently? I don' know, maybe. If you're in my neighborhood, whether White or Black, the police are going to stop you. If you're White you're buying, if you're Black you're dealin'. Usually they just tell the White kid to go home. But Blacks are always being questioned and harassed. I don't know if I believe all this, but I think this is the way most people in my neighborhood feel.

Debra:

It is hard to say, I don't see many Whites around this area to see if they get treated differently. I don't think many of my hommies would know either. As for all cities, I think most people would agree that Blacks are harassed more. That's why so many brothers are in prison. I think most people would say that police watch for Blacks to commit more crimes, and follow more Blacks around waiting for them to sell drugs, or rob some store to buy dope. I think most cops think young Black boys are dealing drugs.

Although, Debra had reported not seeing the different ways Whites and Blacks are treated by the police, she articulated the very concerns that had been previously explicated in the works of Baldwin (1962), Samaha (1994), and Williams (1993), that of the police patrolling of the Black neighborhoods as a form of institutionalized racism, which becomes an insult and a symbol of White power in Black underclass communities.

Other respondents were more up front and open about the overt racism within the policing agencies, while others talked about the media influence on police decisions and thought processes. Overall, I felt that these respondents had a profound understanding of how racism operates within the policing process.

Other than Red Dog and Sandra who felt that police harassment was more economic than racial, most felt that if you are Black, the police will harass you.

Red Dog:

If you Black they drive by real slow and stare at you, or they'll point at you, harass you. But they dog dirty Whites too. Certain Whites if you're poor they'll harass you. I think it is more money than skin color. They treat everybody in this neighborhood like they sellin' drugs, Black or White.

Sandra:

I think they harass more Blacks than they do Whites around here. If a group of Whites be hangin' on the corner they don't stop and ask them what they doin' or nothing. Like if a group of young Blacks are together they always stop and ask if we sellin' drugs. That's bull shit. But they treat the, what do they call them? White trash had too. So maybe it ain't all 'cause we Black. It might be 'cause we poor. I doubt they hassle the people on the north side the way they harass this area.

Still the rest were not so willing to give social class that much power. Most agreed that it was a racial issue rather than an economic issue. However, I believe that most of my respondents would have considered social class as an issue, had I given them the opportunity to respond in that fashion. It would have been very interesting to see how many of the respondents would have made social class the most salient issue when discussing policing procedures. It is very interesting that both Red Dog and Sandra pointed out the dynamics of social class. Both talked about how Blacks are harassed and watched in their community, but once they started thinking about poor Whites, they began to express ideas of classism and expound on that thought by explaining how poor Whites may be treated similar to poor Blacks.

Some of the other respondents answers gave illustrations of, and talked about, overt racism among police officers.

Tenise:

Yeah. I think the police bother the Blacks more than Whites. They think if you young and Black, you probably sellin' drugs. So they always keeping their eyes on you. You can't walk down the street without a cop wanting to know what you doin'. I don't know how they treat Whites. It's hard to say, but I know they dog the Blacks around here.

Shelia:

Some police are racist. If a Black person gets shot they always assume it had to be drug related. They don't know if it is drug or gang related, they just assume. They also assume that Whites are sellin' or in gangs because Blacks pull them in.

Kaye:

Yes, it's like if three or more Black guys are hangin' on the corner, just out of school, gettin' off the bus. They'll pull up and harass them just because of stereotypes. Thinkin' it's gotta be a gang. Or, four or more deep in a car, Black guys, they'll pull 'em over. It could be four kids goin' to Azars, goin' to work. They'll pull 'em over. That's basically what I see.

Education, is another institution which inner-city Black males and females have lost respect for. And one does not question why after reading Jonathan Kozol's book *Savage Inequalities*. According to Kozol (1991), "In public schooling, public policy has been turned back almost one hundred years" (p. 4). His book investigates the conditions of schools in inner-cities and compares them to the suburban school districts in the same area. What he found was that schools in inner-cities were poorly funded, lacked the resources needed for teaching, lacked lab equipment and updated books, and were typically unpleasant to look at and visit. The poorly funded schools were typically predominately Black, and were surrounded by no drug zone signs, guards at the doors and guards walking the halls, and an absence of quality teachers, or an absence of teachers period. Some days children showed up to a classroom to find they had no teacher (Kozol, 1991). Kozol visited cities like East St. Louis, Illinois, New York, New York; Camden, New Jersey; and Santonio, Texas. He eventually came to the conclusion that this is yet another form of institutionalized racism. He felt that these children could not get an education in these poor environments, therefore, they would eventually drop out; and obviously were ill prepared to complete in the legitimate economy.

While participation in the community leads me to believe that Fort Wayne has no high schools nearly as bad as those mentioned in Kozol's book, education remains a key issue when discussing institutionalized racism, drugs, and crime. If we do not give our children a quality education, so that they can lead healthy and productive lives, society will pay later in violence and other economic costs (Kozol, 1991).

According to Taylor (1990) this lack of quality education has lead youth to giving up on achieving their dreams through legitimate means. Historically, those who leave school are the ones who are more likely to end up in gangs. "From 1976 to 1984 African-Americans lost 56,000 students before graduating from high school.

The drop out rate is a clear indication of frustration felt by students, their families, and educators" (Taylor, 1990, p. 94). In the *Invisible Man* (1947), Ralph Ellison illustrates how the African-American is ignored, disrespected, and treated as less than human in American society. "Sociologists Ohlin and Cloward theorized about blocked opportunities and Merton underlined `the ends justify the means' as a major and ruling factor in the American dream" (Taylor, 1990, p. 94).

One of the teachers in Kozol's book read these words of Langston Hughes to her class:

What happens to a dream deferred?

Does it dry up?

Like a raisin in the sun?

She reported, after reading this to her class, that the class began to cry. She was fired the next day, and was told that the poetry she was reading to the class was regarded as flammatory (Kozol, 1991), p. 2).

Although the Fort Wayne schools appear to be of high quality compared to those mentioned in Kozol's book (1991), the respondents still had a negative attitude about school and school administrators. Seven of the respondents I surveyed went to South Side high school. A school which has remarkably low drop out rates for an inner city school, and is currently under going gentrification. However, the Fort Wayne school board is going to construct new boundaries for those who will attend South Side high school when the transformation is complete, and it will probably send south central residents to a more poorly equipped Elmhurst high school (this was hearsy reported from some students who have attended and are attending South Side high school).

Although seven of the respondents graduated from high school, one reported going to college, the respondents still felt unprepared to compete in the legitimate economy. This is exemplified in their statements about alternatives to, and opportunities within, the formal economy. Many have reported, as seen earlier in their responses, that employers won't hire people like them. I am assuming they are not only referring to their skin color, but their level of education as well. Even those who have graduated from high school report only being qualified to do entry level work, and that employers do not trust them. In the specific questions directed towards school, they continue to reply that they are not getting an education that will prepare them for the future, nor does the educational system teach them how to deal with real life on the streets. I asked the respondents how they think their friends would respond to the following statement: I think school is important to help youth get ahead. Why? Why not? These are the responses:

Red Dog:

Most people I know have a bad attitude about school. They can't get nothing out of it, so who really cares? They don't learn nothin' that prepares them to make money. Now if they had a class on how to sell drugs, every kid in the school would attend. That's a class they could learn something from.

Sandra:

Mostly school is a waste. The teachers don't care nothing about us. Most people either skip, or just sit in class doin' nothing. They don't take notes, nothing. They know school is bullshit. It has nothing to do with the real world.

Tenise:

I don't think anyone really thinks they gettin' anything out of school. Sure there are some who study and stuff, but I think they know it's a joke too. School doesn't teach you about real life. All it prepares you for is a minimum wage job. They need to teach you how to survive living on the streets. That's what really needs to be taught in schools-how to survive the street without gettin' killed.

Stelia:

Waste of time, most do not use what is learned. Most don't try to do anything with what they learn. They get kicked out and never return. They rebel by not coming back. They don't see school as helping them with their future. They'd rather be out selling, living the high life. You don't need school. School don't teach you how to sell drugs.

Temika:

Most see school as useless. It don't teach you nothing about how to make money and survive. Most people, that I know, have high school diplomas and can't even find a job. Why waste your time in school when you could be out on the streets makin' real money by selling or stealing?

Theresa:

School is not important. They see quick ways to get ahead, so the don't think they need an education. They don't realize how much you can get out of an education.

Kaye:

No, because I think once they start sellin' drugs and they get a taste of that money, everything else goes by the wayside. The younger boys, like eighteen and under, they start sellin' drugs, and they see the money they can make, nothin' else is important, 'cause they think that money is all there is in life; that's what's important.

Dieonne:

I see some kids, they play around, like I can take my nephew for example, he didn't think school was important. He'd fuck off and get in trouble.

Denise:

Most kids today don't have any respect for school 'cause it ain't teaching them how to live in the real world. What we have to deal with out here is not taught in no school books. Most kids know that they don't need school to sell drugs.

Debra:

No I doubt it. I know when I was in school I thought it was stupid. I didn't get nothing out of it. I think most kids today feel the same way. School really has nothing to do with real life.

Similar responses were resonated when asked if they thought the school teachers and administrators were there to help. Nine out of the ten respondents said that most, or all of them, don't care about getting the students an education. Most felt that the administrators and teachers would get paid whether they teach the students something or not. Kaye, who was not a gang number, felt that every school was different, and that every individual gets something different out of school. Therefore, she felt she could not answer that question.

Welfare as Deviance

Attitudes toward welfare was another area not explicitly designed in the research but with strong ties to the informal economy. I first asked the respondents if they felt welfare was necessary. Secondly, I asked them about alternatives to welfare in their community. The positive reception of welfare and the perception of the lack of alternatives supports my hypothesis that these Black females have assumed the role of the innovator as a response to anomie as set forth by Merton (1938).

All ten respondent's agreed that welfare was necessary. All the respondents also agreed that within their community welfare was an accepted way of taking care of your family. No one dissed (disrespected) women on welfare: "they do what they have to do."

Shelia:

Yes, you get the money the best way you know how. A lot of women have babies so they can get welfare. But they have to quit after four, `cause you get no additional money after the fourth child.

Theresa:

Yes welfare is necessary. If not on welfare most women would work in restaurants, as CNA's, or any other entry level job. Some people do abuse the welfare system, but most women use it to get ahead. Like me, I'm going to school and trying to become something so I can be a role model for my kids. When I get my degree I can get off welfare. I'm not going to work for minimum wage when I can stay home and spend time with my children.

Kaye:

In my neighborhood all the women I know are on, and I'll say all, only time it differs is when the girl has a baby under age, and then she on it under her mom. Other than that it is very necessary, `cause that's what's supportin' their habit. All of the drugs are sold at the first of the month. Very necessary. Alternatives to welfare? If they said we will give you food, but for everything else you got to work. But, they don't say that, either work or don't get. I mean I don't at this point, but if I was usin' and had children, I can't have children at this point, but if I could, I'd have four or five babies, because that's an easy way to keep your supply comin' in, you know at the first of the month you gettin' that check. And you can do whatever you want during the month, `cause you know every month the government goin' to be there at your door with a paycheck for ya'. I lived in a house where that's all they did, have three or four kids and they would pay them to run drugs out of their house a couple of days and they could stay rent free the rest of the month.

123

Dieonne:

To a certain degree. See, with me, I got three children, and when I get them back, I don't intend to be on welfare, I can go out and work. But for those who can't, for those who need assistance, it's necessary. But for those who can go out and get a job, I don't know why they should rely on welfare.

Denise:

Most women in this area are collecting welfare and sellin' dope out of their houses. It is kind of dangerous when you got kids, so some they just live off their welfare checks. I don't know of any jobs around here for women where they can make as much money as they do off of sellin' crack. I think a lot of women be smart when they collect welfare 'cause they get all the benefits. Most women who work don't get any health insurance for their kids, so they just never take their kids to the doctor. If a kid gets sick they end up sellin' a little on the side anyways to pay the doctor bills. Most women in this neighborhood get welfare 'cause they care about feedin' and taking care of their kids. That's the only way to do it. Ain't nobody going to hire us for much more than minimum wage, and if they do they say it's part time, work ya' forty hours a week, and don't give you any health care plan. Also, it cost a lot of money to have someone watch your kids while you are at work. If you're dealing or on welfare, the kids can stay with you.

When responding to the question of available alternatives to welfare, nine out of ten responded that there were no alternatives to welfare; they conclude that there were no jobs, at least high paying jobs available for people like them. These responses clearly illustrate the lack of alternatives that are necessary for the innovator to adapt illegitimate means to achieve desired success. If there truly are no jobs, or at least that is the perception of Black females in this community, it would be naive of us to think that women in this neighborhood would not find different (collecting welfare) or illegitimate alternatives to get money. The following quotes are some of the responses to the perceived alternatives to welfare.

Red Dog:

A lot of women are on welfare and sellin' drugs. Neither one pays high enough so they got to do both. Most women around here don't like to leave their children and go to work. They can't find work anyway.

Sandra:

No one can find a job in this neighborhood, especially if you got kids. You can't afford to pay someone to watch them. Most women around here collect welfare, and sell drugs for their man, 'cause he is too strung out to do it himself. This one check supports her man's habit by sellin' drugs for him. How can he pay support when she has to work to buy his drugs? It is sad, but no one blames women on welfare.

Tenise:

There isn't any work around here that pays enough to raise a family, you get to collect welfare. No, sellin' drugs is not seen as an alternative to welfare, but additional incomes on top of their welfare checks.

Temika:

Welfare is usually always collected, if women are sellin' drugs, they're still collecting their welfare checks. A lot of young chicks hide their cadillac on the days the social worker is stopping by, because if they don't the social worker know she's prostitutin' or sellin'. I think most women would much rather sell than prostitute. I think that would be the number one choice for an alternative to welfare.

Theresa:

Not anything that pays more than entry level pay. It makes more sense, if you have kids, to collect welfare. Only if they use it in the wrong way, and don't try to get ahead.

Not all agree that selling drugs is morally right, but most agree that is an alternative for individuals wanting to support themselves in a neighborhood where there is very little work and the work that is available are dead-end, low paying jobs. Kaye mentioned the availability of jobs such as janitorial work, restaurants and McDonald's. Most realized that this type of work will not pay the bills, nor will you get ahead. Welfare is perceived as the only choice for those who have kids, and if you are really innovative not only will you collect welfare, but you will sell drugs as well.

As proposed by Merton, if there are no legitimate opportunities for achieving culturally desired goals a person will adapt in one of four ways which are considered deviant. These alternatives, or adaptations may be viewed as deviant by some members of the larger society, but within particular subcultures, they may be viewed as the only alternative, and not viewed as deviant by other members of their subculture.

Cloward and Ohlin (1960) expanded on Merton's theory by saying that people had different access to legitimate means as well. In an economically oppressed area, where the retreatist lives next to the innovators, one of the obvious means of adaptation to the discrepancy between culturally defined goals and socially prescribed means may be selling drugs. The retreatists do the drugs to forget about their deprivation while the innovators sell drugs to alleviate the stress from deprivation. What is missing from this theoretical approach, however, is the critique of the economic system which negates a group of people who are at the bottom of the socio-economic ladder. In capitalist society Zero sum competition inevitably creates winners and losers, many of these losers strive to enter the winners bracket at whatever cost. Liberal reforms which offer equal access to entering the contest will not solve the problem. The current drug problem will exist as long as there is an unequal economic system. Even if drugs are legalized, the oppressed will find some illegitimate way to make money, It 's survival.

CHAPTER XIII

Conclusion

Historical and Institutionalized Racism

In conclusion, the history of racial oppression has been well documented in the works of Davis (1944/1981), Wilson (1987), Leiman (1993) and Wallace (1990). Historically, the United States has been a racist, male dominated, society. Our founders, and writers of the U.S. Constitution, prided themselves in building a country that would open its boundaries to all people: providing they were of European descent, and that they assimilated quickly into White Anglo Saxon Protestant culture. However, African-Americans did not come to the U.S. by their own choosing, they were brought to the United States from Africa and bought and sold by European land owners. Blatant discrimination after slavery existed in the form of Jim Crow segregation as well as special Black codes that existed in the south. This imperialist, patriarchal mentality left African-American women in a unique position to care for the Black community without legitimate opportunities to gain access to resources that would enable them to fulfill this atypical predicament. Their current political and economic conditions have left them powerless to fight the plight of poverty and violence which has raped their com- munities of life and property (Leiman, 1993).

Today, the economic conditions of the African-American females, and the new political correctness of subtle indirect racism, have made African-American women victims of institutionalized racism. A form of racism that is much more difficult to fight than blatant, overt racism. The poor quality of schools in lower-class communities (Kozol, 1991), coupled with lack of job opportunities within poor urban areas (Leiman, 1993), has led many minorities into the violent milieu of the informal economy. The minority group experience in the United States leads to an investment in the informal economy and, because of shared oppression there is a history of this involvement. The Chinese were trafficking opium (Thomas, 1992), the Mexicans, Marijuana (Musto, 1973), and the Italian mafia's profit making black market was alcohol during the depression. And, more recently, immigrants from Central America and the Caribbean are developing large markets from coca and poppy plants within the economically barren terrains of barrios and ghettos. We can place gang activity and gang violence in the center of this developing underground economy. This black market is enabling a few African-Americans to accumulate large fortunes in otherwise economically disadvantaged communities.

The Black Feminization of Poverty

Having good reason to believe that the Black female is the most effected social category in the current economic and political arrangement, it was incumbent to investigate those economic conditions; and interview women from an economically oppressed community, who have seen, or have had contact with the illegitimate economy; to ascertain attitudes towards their current conditions economically; and, to solicit their views on alternatives to the current legitimate economy.

In Chapter V, I examined the current, and past, economic conditions of African-American females. I would hope at this point that there would be no dispute that they are Truly Disadvantaged. Since 50% of all Black children live below the poverty level (Lawson, 1992), and since things have not changed for African-American women over the past ten years, it is a virtual inevitability that their relationship with the formal economy would foster negative attitudes toward this institution. Leiman (1993) notes that the young Black population is so frustrated by their disproportionately impoverished conditions, that they have stopped actively looking for positions within the formal economy, and are looking for employment within the informal economy.

Economic Oppression and Entry Into the Informal Economy

Previous gang literature has not specifically explored the current economic condition of Black women when assessing their involvement in gang activities, such as selling drugs. It was my assumption that Black females, like their male counterparts, also would like a piece of the American Dream. I found, as Taylor (1993) did, that African-American females are getting involved in the selling and distribution of drugs to make money. However, the women that I interviewed were convinced that most of the young, African-American females involved in gangs, and selling drugs are doing it for the money. They recognized that there were very few options for women like them to make a living. Even with a high school education, most agreed that the only legitimate employment opportunities were entry level, dead end, low-paying jobs.

These research findings are unique in that the respondents discussed the use of welfare in combination with selling drugs. They claimed that both were needed in order to support their community and families. Taylor's (1993) respondents were more interested in personal ambitions than the women in my study. The women I interviewed were still grounded in the traditional family which is a more inherent part of established Black values. They made mention of their roles as mothers and saw selling drugs and collecting welfare as a temporary step toward a middle-class legitimate lifestyle. The women in Taylor's book appear to be more representative of innovator's as discussed in Merton's (1957) work. Female crew members in Detroit appear to have adapted those white middle-class values depicted in Merton's book describing innovator. Although the women I interviewed claimed to know females who could fit the innovator category, few want to maintain that label later in life. Most see innovative behavior as acceptable and necessary, but only for the short run. When I asked the respondents where they see themselves in ten years, most reported wanting to have a job, education, husband, and children. This data may show a time dimension to anomie that Merton (1938) did not discuss. It is possible that those who become innovators to adapt to discrepancies between culturally prescribed goals and legitimate means only take on the innovative status temporarily. Maybe the innovator does not accept this position for long term. This idea will be discussed later in the section for future research.

The people in our society tend to blame the individual when they get involved in unethical, immoral behavior. It is easier to say that those involved in selling drugs are bad people, rather than say that the current economic system is designed so that some people fail, or can not compete in the current job market. This predisposes a certain population of people into the illegal economy. The increase in policing and convictions of drug offenders has resulted in the serious overrepresentation of African-Americans into the criminal justice system (Messner & Rosenfeld, 1994; Samaha, 1994).

Racism and the Criminal Justice System

The illegitimate opportunities present through the illegal drug market have also increased arrest rates and convictions of females. Wilson (1993) argues that this may be a result of African-American females having access to a home or apartment; something that is needed as a base to sell drugs. A home with a telephone, heat, etc.

Women can provide a stable base from which to run their drug business (Wilson, 1993).

Because of reports of increased female criminality and involvement in the sales and distribution of drugs, coupled with their past and current economic conditions, and dependency on welfare, I was curious to see how this population of women constructed their lives. I wanted to know what their attitudes were towards racism, sexism, women selling drugs, welfare, the police and education. These, I felt, were all forms of institutionalized racism which contributed to keeping the urban, African-American, female in an oppressed condition. I wanted to know. Did they understand their current condition, politically, economically and morally? And, were they rationalizing their involvement in gangs and the selling of drugs? Were they aware of their lack of alternatives?

What I discovered from the population of women I interviewed was, that their answers were yes to all of these questions. Their frustration with their current economic conditions was certainly expressed in their discussions with me about the current job opportunities within their community. Most talked about employers not wanting to hire people like them as well as alluding to the fact that the only job opportunities available are those which pay minimum wage. Not only were they concerned about the dead end, low-paying jobs that are available, they were also disturbed by the way they were treated by their employers. They talked about the levels of distrust and being stereotyped as lazy, and even stupid. Most felt that these employment conditions were deplorable and did not inspire them to pursue job possibilities.

Alternatives to Welfare and the Informal Economy

When asked about alternatives to welfare, respondents echoed the same concerns; there were no attractive or adequate jobs for them, and those jobs that are available don't pay enough for child or health care. The majority agreed that welfare was one of the few alternatives to the legitimate work force. None of them blamed women on welfare, because this is the way that these mothers took care of their children and provided them with appropriate medical services. All of the respondents agreed, outside of those who referred to janitorial and service work, that the illegitimate economy was also an alternative for women in the South Central, Fort Wayne area.

So, as policy makers debate the future of welfare services to the poor and deprived, attention must be directed toward providing legitimate jobs to replace the money being made in the informal economy. Jobs must also provide some form of health care, or there must be a national health care plan. It is instructive here to reflect on the reasons for women being on welfare. Many respondents discussed the issue of welfare providing health care. One respondent talked about how it would be stupid for a woman to work a minimum wage job that offers no health care package when a woman can get health care provided while on welfare.

We not only need to replace illegitimate work with legitimate work that provides health care, but we also need to provide legal employment opportunities which retain the lower-class's sense of mastery, control and dignity. Marx argues that human beings express the essence of their humanity through their work. The informal economy represents poor peoples methods for maintaining their humanness, a sense of mastery, and allows them to be productive through accumulating the legitimate unit of exchange money.

Perceptions of Black Female Gang Members

All agreed that women operating within the illegitimate economy were making as much money as their male counterparts, and felt that violence is just a part of the informal economy. However, none of the respondents reported knowing of any all-female gangs. As stated earlier, it is possible that all female gangs are a phenomena of larger cities, or that the recent onset of gang activities in Fort Wayne has not yet lent itself to the separation of male/female gangs. Therefore, my research efforts changed from looking at all female gangs, to gender mixed, and possibly, racially mixed gangs. I did not find women operating their own crews, or acting independently of male gang members. Although, I did find that these women, for the most part, claimed to be operating as equals, and allegedly making as much money as the male gang members. I also discovered that the women I interviewed felt that women in gangs were moving away from what the literature would characterize as stereotypical roles (subservient and marginal) women previously held in gangs, as reported in the works of Rice (1963) and Bowker, Gross and Klien (1980).

However, I don't think the question addressing the equality of female gang members can be dealt with without discussing the different methods of female entrance into gender mixed gangs. As alluded to in the literature, as well as in self reports by my respondents, there are two ways for a female to enter a gang--sexed in or beat in (physically attacked). If you are sexed in you enter the group at a subordinate status. Females who are sexed in will never gain equal status with male members. However, those females that are beat in can gain equality with male members. This is because female members who are sexed in are seen as "hos" (prostitutes - or women who give sexual pleasure freely) and not deserving of equal status in the group. Whereas, those women who are beat in (the traditional rite of passage for male gang members) can eventually earn equal status. Women who are beat in usually come across as hard core women. Where those who are sexed in do not come across in this way. In my sample, I only found one respondent who came across as a hard core gang member and was beat in. What we can conclude from this, is that women who enter the gang in the traditional female way continue to be treated in a stereotypical female way, while women who enter the gang in the way traditionally reserved for males are more likely to gain equal access and equal respect. It is possible that equal status through being beat in represents an alternative to the establishment of all female gangs. It may be temporary or developmental in the absence of a critical mass or other opportunities.

Perceptions of Racism and Sexism

The responses I received on the issue of racism also indicated that this particular group of women felt the oppression of a racially biased society, though not as vividly as expected. The women interviewed were very cognizant of, and were able to articulate, their feelings and concerns over the problems of racism. Many respondents discussed their personal experiences with employers distrust, low self-esteem of Black females, the distrust of Black males, and the differences in the ways Black males treat them as compared to white women. These feelings of inadequacy, because of the combination of racism and sexism in society, have also been transcribed in memoirs by Cooper (1892/1988), Davis (1944/1981), hooks (1981) and Wallace (1990). The responses I received from these self reports of oppression have been previously published by Black feminist scholars.

As with racism, this particular group of females, realized that society in general treats them differently, not only because they are Black, but also because they are female. Many mentioned that they can make as much money as men, and earn the same amount of respect as men, but they have to work much harder to earn it. Many of the respondents discussed having to take on the focal concerns Miller (1958) discussed in order to be respected and to succeed in the informal economy. Women have to get beat in, not sexed in; they have to be willing to use violence; and, they must be as ruthless as males in their business undertakings. To be too feminine would be a detriment. Women who are sexed in are seen as "hos," get no respect, and will never shake this status.

All of the respondents did not trust the police; nor did they think the police were there to help them. Most felt that the police just harass the people in their community. They presumed that the police were racist, because they believe that all Blacks in their area are dealing drugs or, they're stealing. Two respondents denied that this was purely a race issue, but felt the police harassed people in their neighborhood because they were poor.

The sample women in Fort Wayne appeared to be very aware of racial and sexual dynamics as they played themselves out in their personal lives. They made reference to neighborhoods that they were not allowed entrance because of skin color. There were also indications of very sophisticated social class analysis when several of the women made articulated points regarding the police departments and patrol officers hatred of poor people. One of the respondents talked about the police assuming that everyone in her neighborhood must be selling or buying drugs, just because it is a poor community (if you're White you're buying, if you're Black you're selling).

Respondents were also aware of sexual oppression in society as well as within the drug selling, underclass communities. Many of the women suggest, that while women can be equal to men in drug selling gangs, males are still the movers, shakers and suppliers and probably the real money makers in their community. This is consistent with Taylor's work (1993). Taylor (1993) found, that while female gangs were emerging, men still dominate. Taylor's research also indicates more of a struggle for gender equality, whereas in South Central, Fort Wayne women appear to be more accepting of their subordinate status in the gender hierarchy. This may be the result of women in smaller cities accepting traditional values (family and community) more readily than women who live in larger cities where traditions passed on through extended family are usually abandoned.

Education and Its Contribution to Institutionalized Racism

None of the respondents felt that people in their community could see any practical value in a formal education. Selling drugs does not require a formal, mainstream education. If the school taught people in their community real life skills, maybe education would be seen as important. Not seeing formal education as important, or as a key to your future, combined with high dropout rates, also increases the chances of minority youth entering gangs (Taylor, 1990). The women I interviewed, seven out of 10, had high school diploma, and one was registered in college, felt that education has not qualified them for anything but entry level work. These women also addressed the lack of concern by teachers and administrators. They felt the teachers and administrators were there only to get a paycheck.

Problems with Education and some Solutions

Interviewees reported that they felt that most of the people in their neighborhoods did not feel that education was important. Nor did they think that administrators and teachers cared about the quality of education they were receiving. These are similar concerns that Kozol (1991) and Taylor (1990/1993) expressed in their books. Where do we go from here? If we continue to build more prisons and cut social welfare programs and education funding, things can only get worse (Samaha, 1994). New policies are designed to increase police patrol and build more prisons, but by spending more money on prisons and police patrols, our government is only taking potential funding from other program solutions and institutional responses. It isn't completely clear to those with social power that there is an inverse relationship between education and criminality, and that lack of education can also increase the numbers of youth entering the informal economy. Or is it?

It is possible that Black urban youth are sending us a message that the education they are receiving doesn't work and we ought to pay attention to them. But, we should not abandon the responsibility to teach them about the formal economy and what they need to know to be successful, information they may not be aware of. There needs to be a collaboration between teachers and learners about the methods most appealing and instructive to impart this education.

When one examines the high school graduation rates within the prison population, it is shockingly below that of the national average. Of all male prisoners, only 40% have a high school education, and a college graduate in prison is almost unheard of. For the female prison population, only 25% have graduated from high school (Samaha, 1994). When will policy makers understand the impact of not educating the children has on other social institutions? If the respondents from my survey, as well as those from Taylor's (1990) research, feel that the education they are getting is a waste of time, isn't it about time that as a society we take a look at how we are educating our children? We need to ask ourselves, what kind of educational experience would be most effective for Black, inner-city youth? Without solving the education crisis, we will not solve the welfare, or crime crisis in our society (Kozol, 1991). Putting money into the public educational system could seriously reduce the amount of money the society spends for welfare and crime. It concerns me immensely, after reading Kozol's book (1991), that American education has come to this. We are neglecting our societal responsibility to educate a significant portion of our population (Kozol, 1991). And without the appropriate education, how do we expect these youth to compete in or even enter the legitimate economy?

The Lack of Legitimate Opportunities

The lack of societal institutions ability to provide equal opportunities for the pursuit of goal attainment among women and ethnic minorities has been a major concern of classical as well a contemporary sociologists. However, as mentioned earlier, I believe that Merton's structural strain model is by far the most powerful theoretical interpretation of deviance among female gang members in lower-class communities. In the literature review chapters I established a relationship between the social structure, the economy and crime. What remains to complete Merton's theoretical model is the interviewees' evaluations of their current economic situation. Do they feel that they have no alternatives to make money outside of welfare and crime? Three questions specifically addressed these current economic frustrations. The first question I asked was: why do people in your neighborhood get involved in selling drugs? All ten respondents either answered that there ain't no jobs out here or it's for the money. These responses were alluded to when answering the research questions about sexism and racism. It is apparent that the group that I interviewed do not feel that there are enough good paying legitimate jobs for Black females in their community for survival let alone sufficient enough to fulfill the American dream. They feel welfare is a reasonable alternative for women in their neighborhoods who are trying to feed their babies; who can blame them for doing what they have to, to feed the babies?

This supports the theoretical conclusion that the innovators are frustrated with the legitimate economy and will find alternatives (legitimate means--welfare and/or illegitimate means--drug dealing) to succeed. This particular group of women are definitely frustrated with the legitimate economic alternatives. Now to address the second response to anomie. Do these women really find alternative means to achieve societal goals?

If we conclude that welfare is widely considered a deviant means to goal attainment and the same is true of selling drugs, than we can assign the endorsement of both means (welfare being legitimate, but deviant and the selling of drugs being illegitimate) of goal fulfillment as deviant by current cultural standards. Since these women report use and approval of one or both as appropriate forms of economic survival and advancement, it is accurate to assert that they have become innovators as a form of adapting to the frustration experienced because of the discrepancy between goals and means. It is possible to conclude that this group of underclass women have accepted these forms of deviance as legitimate means to achieve socially prescribed goals that are unattainable. In accepting the rationales forwarded by these innovative, yet deviant, means as legitimate ways of attaining the cultural goals of American society, they have demonstrated the level of acceptance urban underclass communities have of the innovator. What is seen as deviant by the larger social structure may now become an accepted form of adaptation to a social structure which denies them access to legitimate means to goals attainment.

A Final Reflection

Given the nature of our state of understanding of this phenomenon and our need for richer detailed insight, this research effort has brought to light something that a positivistic, quantitative study would lose in the numbers. Categorizing people from the sample population and variables in the formal generalization process causes scholars to lose sight of the variability of the individual response experienced as a member of a particular racial, socio-economic and political group. My approach is consistent with McCrea and Markle (1989), who write, "...some sociologists assume a phenomenological approach in which society is the result of people, individually or collectively, interpreting and constructing their realities" (p. 167). Although positivist theory and method are useful, they should not be used exclusively and certainly not initially because of their nonreactive objective. Positivism denies readers access to an understanding of how actors respond to larger social classifications (McCrea & Markle, 1989).

There are a number of ways in which the present study is unique, and therefore offers valuable contributions to the field of sociology. While there is extant research on female gang members, it fails to combine feminist ideologies, political-economic considerations, and the oppressive conditions which deny these women access to the formal economy and which therefore predispose them to take on the role of the innovator, as described in Merton's (1938) model.

This research has gained insight into the way in which a carefully defined sample of women interpret their world. Without the techniques employed and data resulting from this research we would not have known of: The participation of females in equal status in mixed gender gangs dealing in the informal economy, the distinction between being sexed in and beat into a gang, the combination and legitimation of drug dealing and welfare, the possibility of a temporary dimension to innovation, and the relationship of all these to the previous racism and sexism in society. Studies stimulated by these findings need to be duplicated in many different places to help our understanding of the changes in the larger political-economy and the consequences for poor and historically oppressed people.

This is the only research that looks specifically at female gang members in a small to medium size urban area. The differences between what has been found here and what has been discovered in larger cities have created new research questions addressed in the section "future research."

Future Research

Throughout the findings and conclusion chapters I have pointed to evocative findings and theoretical opportunities for future research. First of all, it is important to make note of the lack of all-female gangs in the Fort Wayne area. Is this the result of a lack of critical mass or perhaps cultural lag? It is important in the future to investigate the discrepancies between my findings and Taylor's (1993). The only way to address this question is to conduct research in systematically selected small and medium sized cities where gang activity is known to be well established or known to be a recent phenomenon.

Second, in gender mixed gangs, there are conflicting views on whether females in gangs can have equal status with males. It appears from this research that if female gang members enter the gang in the fashion of their male counterparts, they either enter with equal status, or claim that equality is obtainable. Those females who are sexed in, however, can apparently never gain equal status. Also, we may investigate if entrance into a gender mixed gang in a way traditionally reserved for males by a female may operate as an alternative in areas where all female gangs are not in existence. Longitudinally, we may investigate if mixed-gender gangs are a step toward the development of a female autonomous gang.

Third, it is important to investigate the level at which Black female gang members are participating in the informal economy through selling drugs, not only as an alternative but, in addition to receiving welfare. The coexistence of these two modes is an interesting finding that requires more explicit investigation. Perhaps, Black females are turning to welfare for a stable income, while selling drugs to supplement their monthly government check. If so, what becomes the primary activity? Is it age or era related?

And finally, it is important to investigate the possible time dimension aspect of the innovator. Do these women only see themselves as innovators temporarily? How is this different from the total acceptance of the innovator status for male gang members, and possibly female gang members in larger urban areas? It appears that the residents in South Central, Fort Wayne have not given up on achieving conventional values and lifestyles. Is it possible that females who have taken on the innovator status in smaller cities don't lose sight of conventional values because they are never completely removed from or isolated from people who actively pursue

142

conventionality or ritualistic responses? In larger cities, on the other hand, we may investigate whether it is easier for Black females to be more completely isolated from the conventional social values. Thus, in larger cities perhaps there is restricted access to conventional roles.

We also need to know more about the workings of the informal economy and the role that it plays in the survival strategies for poor, underclass people. The phenomological approach helps us to study people individually and therefore we can more thoroughly interpret the way they construct their lives (Gouldner, 1974).

Regretted Research Limitations

In order to have realized the potential of this research, I would have needed to live in the South Central, Fort Wayne area. I would have needed to deepen my knowledge of the residents and the community. Because of the inevitable limitations of the dissertation, and my residence one hour north of Fort Wayne, the time and resources for a detailed ethnography were not available. That would be a research project that would require greater resources and years of investigation. However, I am gratified with the willingness and openness of the women I interviewed and the valuable insights they provided. And I would like to take this opportunity to thank them for their time, honesty and their contribution.

APPENDIX A

SEMI-STRUCTURED INTERVIEW QUESTIONNAIRE

BACKGROUND INFORMATION:

    A.   Socio-economic status of respondent's community:

        1. Where do you live?

        2. What High School did you attend, or would you have attended?

    B. Respondent's demographics:

        1. What was the last grade you completed in school?

        2. How old are you?

        3. Do you have any children?

        4. Are you married?

        5. In the family that you grew up in, was there a Mother and Father both present? If no: Mother only? Father only? If no, what was the arrangement?

COMMUNITY LEVELS OF GANG ACTIVITIES:

    1. Would you say there are a lot of identifiable gangs in the area? If yes, what types of gangs? gangs that sell drugs? Do drugs? Territorial type gangs?

    2. Do you know of any gangs that females lead? All female gangs (no male members)? If yes, what type of activities are these females involved in? Would you say female gangs are as violent as male gangs? Would you say female gangs are making a lot of money off of the sale of drugs?

PERCEIVED COMMUNITY LEVELS OF DRUG USE AND DRUG SALES:

1. Why do you think people in your community get involved in selling drugs?

PERCEIVED LEVELS OF COMMUNITY VIOLENCE:

1. Do you think a lot of females are carrying guns in your neighborhood? If yes, why do you think this is so?

2. Would you say there are a lot of women who get into fights in your neighborhood? If yes, do you think these fights are drug related? If so, why?

INSTITUTIONAL PERSPECTIVES AND ACTIVITIES:

A. Attitudes toward school officials:

    1. Would most of your friends agree with the following statement: I think school is important to help youth get ahead. Why, why not?

    2. Would your friends agree or disagree that most principals and teachers are there to help students? Why, why not?

B. Policing:

    1. Would most of your friends agree that the police are there to help? Why, why not?

C. Attitudes Toward Police and the Criminal Justice System:

    1. Have you ever heard your friends refer to the police as racist? Do they ever blame their arrest or being harassed because they are Black? Do they feel that people of color get the same treatment as whites?

    2. Do you think women get treated differently by the police in your community? Why, why not? Do you think Black women are treated differently by the police than white women? Why, why not?

D. Attitudes toward welfare:

    1. Do most people in your area see welfare as necessary?

2. What are some alternatives to welfare in your neighborhood? Do most people feel that women on welfare could find some other source of income if they wanted to?

PERCEPTIONS OF THE NATURE OF SOCIETY:

A. Sexism in Society:

1. Do you think that women get the same respect as men in your community? Society in general? Why? Or, why not?

2. Do you think women who sell drugs get the same respect as men who sell drugs? Why? Or, why not?

B. Racism in Society:

1. Do you think that people in your neighborhood are racist? Is Society as a whole racists? Do you think Black females have different experiences in life compared to White Females?

C. Attitude Towards the Legalization of Drugs:

1. Do you think drugs should be legalized? If yes, all or only some? which ones?

D. Attitudes Toward the Future:

1. What do you see yourself doing in ten years?

2. What do you see your friends doing in ten years?

APPENDIX B

SLANG GLOSSARY

Beastmaster - the person in the group or gang responsible for violence.

(Beemer - BMW)

Benzo - Mercedes Benz

Crack - mixture consisting usually of cocaine, lidocaine, and baking soda, but often consisting of unknown chemicals

Crackhead - compulsive user of crack cocaine or freebase

Crew - gang, group of associates who come together for business or pleasure

Def - exquisite; the ultimate

Dick - a penis

Dissed (dissing) - showing disrespect or being disrespectful

Doggin' (dogged) - preforming sex acts for money

Dope - someone or something that is very admirable

Dough(ski) - money

Fake - to be a phony

Fresh - someone or something that is very admirable; to look good or to compliment someone

Head - oral sex

Heater - a gun

Ho(es) - whore

Homeboy (homie) - a close friend or companion

Hustler - a person who lives by his or her wits

Illin' - to act obnoxious

Packing (strapped) - carrying a weapon

Paper - money

Posse - an organized group of teens

Rolling - the act of selling narcotics

Skeezer - a female that sleeps with men for money or dope; sometimes refers to women in general

Vette - a corvette

Zero - a person crazy enough to shoot and kill anyone

APPENDIX C

TRANSCRIBED INTERVIEWS

Background Information

Name of respondent's (many names have been changed to protect the respondent).

Respondent # 1 (Red Dog)

Respondent # 2 (Sandra)

Respondent # 3 (Tenise)

Respondent # 4 (Shelia)

Respondent # 5 (Temika)

Respondent # 6 (Theresa)

Respondent # 7 (Kaye)

Respondent # 8 (Dieonne)

Respondent #9 (Denise)

Respondent #10 (Debra)

A. Socio-Economic Status of Respondent's Community:

    1. Where do you live?

        All respondent's live in the area that I have defined as South Central Fort Wayne.

    2. What High School did you attend?

        Respondent #1 - South Side High School

        Respondent #2 - South Side High School

        Respondent #3 - South Side High School

        Respondent #4 - South Side High School

        Respondent #5 - South Side High School

        Respondent #6 - Anthis Career Center

Respondent #7 - Paul Harding High School

Respondent #8 - Elmhurst High School

Respondent #9 - South Side High School

Respondent #10- South Side High School

B. Respondent's demographics:

    1. What was the last grade completed in school?

       Respondent #1 - 11

       Respondent #2 - 11

       Respondent #3 - 12

       Respondent #4 - 12

       Respondent #5 - 12

       Respondent #6 - 13

       Respondent #7 - 11

       Respondent #8 - 12

       Respondent #9 - 12

       Respondent #10- 12

    2. How old are you?

       Respondent #1 - 25

       Respondent #2 - 22

       Respondent #3 - 24

       Respondent #4 - 21

       Respondent #5 - 19

       Respondent #6 - 33

       Respondent #7 - 30

       Respondent #8 - 31

       Respondent #9 - 23

       Respondent #10- 22

3. Do you have any children?

> Respondent #1 - No
>
> Respondent #2 - Yes (2)
>
> Respondent #3 - No
>
> Respondent #4 - No
>
> Respondent #5 - No
>
> Respondent #6 - Yes (3)
>
> Respondent #7 - No
>
> Respondent #8 - Yes (3, 4 'cause I put one up for adoption when I was 16)
>
> Respondent #9 - No
>
> Respondent #10- No

4. Are you married?

> Respondent #1 - No
>
> Respondent #2 - No
>
> Respondent #3 - No
>
> Respondent #4 - No
>
> Respondent #5 - No
>
> Respondent #6 - No
>
> Respondent #7 - No
>
> Respondent #8 - No
>
> Respondent #9 - No
>
> Respondent #10- No

5. In the family that you grew up in was there a Mother and a Father both present? If no, what was the arrangement?

Respondent #1 - Lived for a while with her mother in Fort Wayne and then moved with her father in Chicago and then moved back to Fort Wayne with her mother when she was 15 years old.

Respondent #2 - Lived with her mother and father until they split up when she was in third grade. She then was raised by only her mother.

Respondent #3 - She was raised by her father all her life. She has never really talked to her mother.

Respondent #4 - She lived in Syracuse, N.Y. with her grandmother until 5th grade and then she lived with her mother in Fort Wayne, where she has resided every since.

Respondent #5 - She was raised by her mother all her life, the summer of her seventh grade year she live with her father in Detroit. Then when school started she moved back with her mother in Fort Wayne.

Respondent #6 - Lived with Mother

Respondent #7 - Mother and Father both present

Respondent #8 - I was raised in a one parent home, I was raised by a friend of my mothers.

Respondent #9 - I was raised by my Mother, My father left when I was around three years old. I think he is living in the Detroit area.

Respondent #10 - I was raised by my Mother. She raised five kids as a single parent, and did everything she could for us. She was a hard worker.

PERCEIVED COMMUNITY LEVELS OF GANG ACTIVITIES:

1. Would you say there are a lot of identifiable gangs in the area where you live? If yes, what types of gangs? What activities are they involved in?

Respondent #1 - Around this area, in here, Between Lafayette and Wayne Trace, over to Lewis there's about 12 to 13 gangs. All the different types are together. Of all gangs, all sell drugs, all gang bang, all of them do the same thing, if you need money you got to keep them there with your folks, you got to do it all to make money. Some of them organize to make money, some organize and decide to make money. You got to keep the money with the hommies, if you need money you do what you gotta do.

Respondent #2 - Around this area Lafayette to Wayne Trace, Lewis to about Paulding about 12 to 13. These cats in these gangs do it all they sell, they bust heads, they makin' money, whatever it takes to survive. You gotta make money. No one gonna give us no jobs, so we gotta do what we have to make money.

Respondent #3 - I don't think there're that many gangs around here, maybe six or eight. They all be doin' everything. They get in fights over territories, the sell drugs to support their house. Today, most gang members live together, instead of at home. They got to pay for their house. I think this is why a lot of them sellin' drugs. When I was in a gang we lived with our parents and just hung together. These kids are living together now. They have to sell to pay their bills. They have to have a car, lights, and groceries. They get into fights, because they have to protect their sellin' territory. I think they originally organize as friends and then, because of a bad family life they moved in together and then they have to start sellin' 'cause they find they can't get a decent job to support themselves.

Respondent #4 - I think there are about three or four different types of gangs in this area. The CPT's, Vice Lords and Black Gangster Disciples. It's a combination of drug sellers, gang bangers, and territory gangs. Its all kinds of gangs together.

Respondent #5 - I think there are about five or six identifiable gangs in this area. I'm not sure what they all do. I know most of them sell drugs to keep the gang goin' and gang bangin' is just a part of the drug sellin' business.

Respondent #6 - Yes, I think there are two different gangs. The gangs are both territorial and drug selling gangs together.

Respondent #7 - yes, two I think, yeah two in our neighborhood and they both have their territories. It wasn't like, depending on if one was on one side and the other on the other corner, or one stood on one side of the street and the other was on the other side of the street, you had to decide what side of the street you goin' to walk on. They are both territorial and drug sellin' gangs.

Respondent #8 - not when I was growin' up, but now I would say that there are a lot of gangs and violence stuff. The gangs are both [territorial and drug sellin'].

Respondent #9 - Yes. I would say there are about six or eight gangs. Most of them are selling drugs, violence, gang bangin', fightin' over territory just becomes a part of it.

Respondent #10 - Yes. I would say there are about eight or nine gangs. I can't say what they do. All I know is the gang members I know be dealin' drugs, they only fight when someone messes up the money, or a rival gang tries to take over drug territory.

2. Do you know of any gangs that females lead? Do you know of any all female gangs? If yes, what type of activities are these female members involved in? Would you say female gangs are as violent as male gangs? Would you say female gangs are making a lot of money off the sales of drugs?

Respondent #1 - No female gangs, males and females run together. They may call themselves G's but they still BGD's. Both male and females sale the drugs. Who ever want to do it can. some are makin' as much money. It's the way you want to do it. It depends on if you just sale to who you know or branch out. But I think the female members are makin' as much money. Most ain't using the drugs. They just tryin' to make ends meet. They ain't makin' a lot of money. The people be flashin' stuff around makin' a lot, but you don't see much of that around here. Anyone sellin' drugs got to be violent, even if they female. It is part of doin' business.

Respondent #2 - I don't know of any gangs that are just female, but there're a lot of female gang members. They do the same thing male gang members do. If they want to sell drugs, they sell drugs. Sometimes I think women are better at sellin' drugs, 'cause people trust them to be honest. I guess the females would be as violent. I saw this one chick kick this dudes ass 'cause he owed her some money. If a bitch is really into dealing she'll carry a gun and ain't afraid to use it, just like the guys. Some girls make lots of money, but most just gettin' by. They sell what they have to make ends meet. Most drug dealers I know just sell to people they know. You make big money when you start sellin' to whoever wants drugs, but you can get busted that way too.

Respondent #3 - No female gangs, they all hang together, males and females. If females sellin' drugs they got to be violent. A lot peoples take advantage of ya if you ain't willin' to use force. Someone think you weak they goin' take from ya'. Even if you female, you got to be willin' to shoot. Some females makin' good money, but it's hard to tell, most females don't flash their money around like male gang members. They try not to be as flashy. But I did know this one chick who drove a Benz while she was on welfare. Everyone knew that ho was dealin'. So I guess there are some women out there makin' dough.

Respondent #4 - Females are only the heads of other females. They're called G' queens. They usually go with one of the guys, or back up the men when they dealing drugs. Yes, women are as violent as men. They fight each other, they fight guys, sell drugs, wear the colors, they do everything the guys do. I don't think the females are makin' as much money as the guys. They usually don't sell as long 'cause they get robbed more, or they get pregnant and go on welfare.

Respondent #5 - No all female gangs that I know of, but female gang members do everything the guys do. They beat each other up, they fight guys over drugs, they carry guns, sell drugs. Usually they working for their man. She usually doesn't make much money 'cause she got some man that she gives it to or spends it on. Most women are soft when it comes to a man he can talk her out of anything. Then they get pregnant and have to stop sellin' 'cause it ain't right to raise a kid in a drug house.

Respondent #6 - No female gangs in my neighborhood. There are female gang members, but not running anything. They usually don't carry guns. I think a lot of the females are carrying knives. Usually females get in fights over gang territory, not so much over drug sales.

Respondent #7 - No. The females I know in gangs are girl friends of the gang members, so they considered themselves part of. For the most part, I see the females drug sellin'

Respondent #8 - No. No female headed gangs

Respondent #9 - No. I wouldn't say there are any female gangs, but there're a lot of females involved in gangs. They sell drugs just like the guys, they'll fight right along side the guys, and they makin' money like the guys. But, if your a girl sellin' drugs, you got to be just as violent as the guys, girls who are soft won't make any money. Guys will take advantage of them.

Respondent #10 - No. I don't know of any gangs that only have girls.

Most the girls run with the guys. They all hang together. There are not a lot of females sellin', but the ones who are, are just as violent and mean, and make just as much money as men. When I was dealin' I knew I had to be tough. Guys think they can get one over on chicks sellin', but no one ever got me. Most women fight over money that's been messed with, or guys, or just over who's sellin' to who. Most girls, if they sell to runners, can make as much money as guys sellin' to the same group. Yeah. I would say they make as much. Sometimes if a girl is pretty, but tough, she can make even more.

PERCEIVED COMMUNITY LEVELS OF DRUG USE AND DRUG SALES:

1. Why do you think young people in your neighborhood get involved in selling drugs?

Respondent #1 - 'cause they ain't givin' nobody out here no jobs. you'll try for couple of months, but ain't no one goin' call you back. Then when you get a job they get snotty with ya' and try to fire ya'. You can make more money on the streets selling drugs. Ain't nobody goin' put up with that stuff for the pay they try to give ya'.

Respondent #2 - They ain't no jobs out here. No one goin' hire someone like me. I ain't never had a job, and ain't no one goin' to give me a chance. Most people around here have to collect welfare or sell drugs, or both. Sometimes when I go in to apply for a job, the manager won't even give me an application 'cause he says I ain't qualified. He don't know shit about my qualifications. I think a lot of young people are forced to sell drugs 'cause there ain't no jobs around here. You certainly can't go to the north side of town and look for a job. They be asking you what your black ass is doin' on that side of town. every time I go to the north side the police stop me 'cause they know I don't belong here. Than when you do get a job the bosses always suspicious thinking you goin' steal something from him, or give something away to your friends. I hate that. They pay you bullshit money, then they constantly harassing ya'.

Respondent #3 - There ain't no jobs for people like me. I don't have enough education or experience to get nothing but a minimum wage job. That's bullshit workin' for minimum wage. It ain't worth it. That's why these cats are out there sellin' drugs. They got to give people like us good paying jobs, or at least a chance to prove we can work hard. Most the time you get hired they already assume you lazy and ain't going to work. I don't like working for minimum wage when they treat you like a criminal. No one has to put up with that. I'd rather collect welfare, or sell drugs. At least when you sellin', you're your own boss.

Respondent #4 - People get involved in selling for the money, attention, to fit in with the older guys. This is the same for females sellers. Actually, the guys prefer females gang members. They don't mess up the money, and when some don't want to pay them they don't back down. Most are selling crack cocaine 'cause that is where you make the most money. You can find crack on any corner. You have to ask who sellin' marijuana, but both males and females can be found selling crack on any street corner in this area.

Respondent #5 - Most people get involved in selling, because it is the only way to make money around here. it is hard to get a job that pays more than sellin'. Most people don't think sellin' crack makes you money, but they're a lot of young people around here who are living on there own and takin' care of their mothers only because of selling crack. They couldn't make that kind of money workin' no minimum wage job. Most people like me can't even get a minimum wage job. They laugh you right out of their business when you ask for an application. It's sad that you can make more money selling drugs, but that's the way it is.

Respondent #6 - 'cause they don't know no better. Someone's got to show them the right way to do things. They don't see other alternatives to selling drugs. They want to make quick money.

Respondent #7 - The younger one's for the most part sell 'cause of what they see of the older one's. They see the cars, the gold, the lifestyle, a lot of them just ain't got no money. And they from broken homes, and nine times out of ten their mothers on crack and they just lookin' for a way out. A majority of them that I see don't use. I think it is mostly about havin' more than what their parents can afford to give 'em. Or they lookin' for a place to belong. They find the family thing in the gang.

Respondent #8 - Yeah. For one thing I can say it's for the money. For example, my mother was a drug dealer and she did it for the money. She got high off of makin' the money. I believe they out there just tryin' to make some money. There ain't any jobs out there for women and for people who you would call disabled. I'm not justifying people sellin', but that's the way it is.

Respondent #9 - I think the biggest thing is the money. They see people around here flashing gold and money and shit, they think they are goin' to make the big bucks. Everybody around here thinks people sellin' dope is makin' money. Besides that, no one is hiring us. If you don't have college and you ain't White, you can't find a job. No offense to you, but I think all employers think Blacks are going to steal from them. Even some of the Black managers treat white workers different. Anyway, who wants to work for minimum wage? That's bullshit.

Respondent #10 - I don't know, maybe it's the money. People who don't have an education can't find any other kind of work. Like, for example, I got off sellin' and now, I can't tell you where I'm workin', but I ain't making no money. I was makin' a lot more sellin' drugs. You spend a lot more on your friends, but you also make a lot more.

PERCEIVED LEVELS OF COMMUNITY VIOLENCE:

1. Do you think a lot of females are carrying guns in your community? If yes, why do you think this is so?

Respondent #1 - Yes, as many as male gang members, for many reasons, mostly to protect themselves, from anything, other gangs, rapist, from anything.

Respondent #2 - A lot of females are carrying guns, 'cause they got to protect themselves. The streets aren't safe anymore. If they selling drugs, they have to protect themselves from, robbers, rapist, rival gangs, whatever is out there.

Respondent #3 - Most carry guns for protection. I bet more females carry guns than males, because it is more dangerous for them. I bet most would be willing to use a gun if they had to. But, most just carry them for protection.

Respondent #4 - Females carry guns for protection, 'cause even guys will shoot females, if ya' can't beat up a female take the easy way out, shoot 'em.

Respondent #5 - They carrying guns 'cause they need to protect themselves from the streets. The streets aren't safe for young girls. But if they carrying guns they have to be willing to use it, or you'll get killed.

Respondent #6 - I don't think they are carrying guns, more knives. People around here think they need protection.

Respondent #7 - No. I don't think gang girls are carryin' anything. I was beat up by some gang girls and they didn't have nothin', they just kicked my ass. They could have cut me, they could have done anything they wanted to. It was eight on one, but they just beat me up.

Respondent #8 - I don't know.

Respondent #9 - Yeah. I think girls are carrying weapons, probably guns. If they are dealing they better be strapped. No one cares if you a guy or a girl when your sellin' they still shoot at ya'. Especially if they think you sold them bad dope or something. It's just dangerous to live around here. You need to protect yourself. The police aren't goin' stop it.

Respondent #10 - Yes. Women are carrying guns. They have to. They could get raped, robbed, beat up, anything. It just makes since to pack a weapon out here. Especially, if your involved in gangs that sell.

2. Would you say there are a lot of women who get involved in fights in your neighborhood? If yes, do you think these fights are drug related? What else is going on?

Respondent #1 - Female gang members fight mostly over drugs, majority fight over drugs, but not always. Some fight 'cause men show them disrespect.

Respondent #2 - most females fight for the same reasons males do. They want people to think they are bad, don't mess with me, I'll kick your ass. In this area you got to build a rep' so no one will mess with you. Once you have a rep' no one going to stiff you on drugs or show you disrespect.

Respondent #3 - Most girls fight to gain a reputation, some fight over drugs and men, but it is usually about protecting your rep'. You have to be tough or people will take advantage of you.

Respondent #4 - women fights are more over gang territory than drugs. females who sell usually don't get into fights. Those who fight are wanna be's.

Respondent #5 - I don't think the fights are drug related, it is more about earning respect. Once you kick somebodies ass no one going to mess with you anymore, not even the guys. Usually you got to fight , or prove you can fight, before you start sellin'. No one wants someone running drugs that ain't willing to beat somebody up over money.

Respondent #6 - I think they get in fights over men and territory. They fight over what space they think is their gang territory.

Respondent #7 - No, I never seen a lot of women fightin'.

Respondent #8 - No, not much violence between women. It's more the men.

Respondent #9 - No. Not to many fights between women. If you get dissed you have to fight, but usually the fights are between men. But women do fight, just not as much.

Respondent #10 - Yeah. Women do fight, but not as much as guys. I had a few girls kick my ass, but that's when I was usin' and sellin' at the same time. They kick my ass 'cause I was usin all the dope I was suppose to sell. I think if women fight, that's usually what it's over, drugs.

INSTITUTIONAL PERSPECTIVES AND ACTIVITIES:

A. Attitudes toward school officials:

1. Would most of your friends agree with the following statement: I think school is important to help youth get ahead. Why, why not?

Respondent #1 - Most people I know have a bad attitude about school. They can't get nothin' out of it so who really cares. They don't learn nothin' that prepares them to make money. Now if they had a class on how to sell drugs, every kid in the high school would attend. That's a class they could learn something from.

Respondent #2 - Mostly school is a waste. The teachers don't care nothing about us. Most people either skip, or just sit in class doin' nothing. They don't take no notes, nothing. They know school is bullshit. It has nothing to do with the real world.

Respondent #3 - I don't think anyone really thinks they gettin' anything out of school. Sure there are some who study and stuff, but I think they know it's a joke too. School doesn't teach you about real life. All it prepares you for is a minimum wage job. They need to teach you how to survive living on the streets. That's what really needs to be taught in schools--how to survive the streets without gettin' killed.

Respondent #4 - Waste of time, most do not use what is learned. Most don't try to do anything with what they learn. They get kicked out and never return. They rebel by not coming back. They don't see school as helping them with their future. They'd rather be out selling, living the high life. You don't need school. School don't teach you how to sell drugs.

Respondent #5 - most see school a useless. It don't teach you nothing about how to make money and survive. Most people, that I know, have high school diplomas and can't even find a job. Why waste your time in school when you could be out on the streets makin' real money by selling, or stealing.

Respondent #6 - School is not important. They see quick ways to get ahead, so they don't think they need an education. They don't realize how much you can get out of an education.

Respondent #7 - No, because I think once they start sellin' drugs and they get a taste of that money everything else goes by the wayside. The younger boys, like eighteen and under, they start sellin' drugs, and they see the money they can make, nothin' else is important, 'cause they think that money is all there is in life, that's what's important.

Respondent #8 - I see some kids, they play around. Like, I can take Gmy nephew for example, he didn't think school was important. He'd fuck off and got in trouble.

Respondent #9 - most kids today don't have any respect for school 'cause it ain't teaching them how to live in the real world. What we got to deal with out here ain't taught in no school books. Most kids know that they don't need school to sell drugs.

Respondent #10 - No. I doubt it. I know when I was in school I thought it was stupid. I didn't get nothing out of it. I think most kids today feel the same way. School really has nothing to do with real life.

2. Would your friends agree or disagree that most the time principals and teachers are there to help students. Why, why not?

Respondent #1 - Out of all the principals, teachers and deans, only two would probably help. No one else cares if they help you, they get paid anyway.

Respondent #2 - Teachers and principals don't care about us. They makin' money doin' nothing. Why should they help us when they make the same amount of money doing nothing. Most that do care, don't get rewarded for it. They're the ones gettin' paid the least. The ones that help don't get paid shit. That just shows that if you don't care, or don't help, you'll make more money.

Respondent #3 - most don't care. They just there making a livin' like everyone else. It's hard to care when the students don't care. No one gives the teachers a break, they hound them all the time. I guess if the students cared the teachers wouldn't be so mean. I guess it works both ways though--if the teachers cared, maybe the students would. But right now, I say most teachers and principals don't care what happens to us.

Respondent #4 - A lot don't care. if teachers think they are there to help, they get no respect. Most students shut teachers out. You can't tell these students nothing. Principals never come out of their office. the whole time I was at South side, I saw a principal two or three times.

Respondent #5 - I don't think to many of them care. They to busy being scared, 'cause the students threaten them all the time. Especially the teachers they know are scared of 'em. It's pretty sad, even if the teachers wanted to care, the students won't let them. They see them as soft, and give them a hard time. some might care, but I think most have gotten so hard, that they can't anymore.

Respondent #6 - No, they don't realize they are there to help. They don't realize how much help they can be.

Respondent #7 - I couldn't answer that, I think it is different for each school and the individual. If some sought out individual attention, and got it, maybe they would think they are helpful, but if you don't look for it. I think it depends on the kid and the teachers, their relationship.

Respondent #8 - Yeah, they would agree. Those that know they are there and want to learn. They would think they are helpful.

Respondent #9 - Some care, but most don't. I wish a teacher or somebody would have talked to me. No one cared what I did in school. I still don't think anyone cares.

Respondent #10 - Maybe, some might care, I would say the majority are just there for a paycheck. I seen to many teachers pass on my friends when they couldn't even read. I know this dude he graduated from high school, and he can't even count money right. People are always makin' fun of him 'cause they can take his money.

B. Policing:

1. Would most of your friends agree that police are there to help? Why, Why not?

Respondent #1 - Police, if you know them they will help, but if you don't, they won't help. Most people around here disrespect the police. Most the time the police just look and harass. They ain't there to help.

Respondent #2 - The police ain't there to help us. They are there to protect the White folks from us. Most the time if we call the police they don't even show.

Respondent #3 - Most people would say the police aren't there to help. It's just like the teachers, they get paid whether they help us or not. They don't give a shit about what happens in this neighborhood. Most people around here don't respect the police. They drive around harass us all the time. They think if you young and black your sellin' drugs. Ain't no one here sellin' drugs.

Respondent #4 - Most hate the police, police are only here to hassle. They see them as trying to stop them from doin' what they see is right. Selling drugs is right for them, and the police just get in the way of business.

Respondent #5 - The police don't help shit around here. They won't even come in this neighborhood unless they driving around real slow staring at us, as if we freaks. Most people don't like police around here. They won't even show up if you call 'em, but they always hangin' around if they see people like me hangin' on a street corner. Cops don't get no respect around here.

Respondent #6 - Police are there to help, but they also feel the police are there to get whatever they can from us. They use are neighborhoods to get ahead, gives them something to do all day.

Respondent #7 - If you're usin' or sellin' they're harassing. They are there to "F" with you, but if your just a residential person tryin' to make ends meet, then they are there to help.

Respondent #8 - Yeah. Today I do, when I was doin', no. Users, they think the police is a bunch of bullshit. I thought they just wanted to be there to try and arrest me and others, and I didn't think they were there to help the community.

Respondent #9 - Most people would say the police ain't there to help. I see them just driving around and staring when some brother be gettin' beat up, but if they think the kid is dealin' they'll stop 'em in a hurry. Even if he ain't dealin', just standin' on the corner, hangin' out with some friends, they'll stop just 'cause they look like they're waitin' to buy.

Respondent #10 - (ha! ha!) None of my friends think the police are there for anything else but to bust some niggahs ass. They just lookin' for a reason to bust someone. They are always drivin' down the road lookin' for someone suspicious. I don't think there is much respect for police in my neighborhood. I don't think police have much respect for us either. I think we both hate each other.

C. Attitudes toward the police and the Criminal Justice system:

1. Have you heard your friends refer to the police as racist? Do they ever blame their arrest or being harassed by the police on their being Black? Do they feel that people of color get the same treatment as whites?

Respondent #1 - If you black they drive by real slow and stare at you, or they'll point at you, harass you. But they dog dirty Whites too. Certain Whites, if you poor they'll harass you. I think it is more money than skin color. They treat everybody in this neighborhood like they sellin' drugs, Black or White.

Respondent #2 - I think they harass more Blacks more than they do Whites around here. If a group of Whites be hangin' on the corner they don't stop and ask them what they doin' or nothing. Like if a group of young Blacks are together they always stop and ask if we sellin' drugs. That's bullshit. But they treat the, what they call them? White Trash bad too. So maybe it ain't all 'cause we black. It might be 'cause we poor. I doubt they hassle the people on the north side the way they harass us in this area.

Respondent #3 - Yeah. I think the police bother the Blacks more than Whites. They think if you young and Black, you probably sellin' drugs, so they always keeping their eyes on you. You can't walk down the street without a cop wanting to know what you doin'. I don't know how they treat Whites, it's hard to say, But I know they dog the Blacks around here.

Respondent #4 - Some police are racists. If a Black person gets shot they always assume it had to be drug related. They don't know if it is drug or gang related, they just assume. They also assume that whites are sellin' or in gangs because Black people pull them in.

Respondent #5 - Yeah, I'd say they are racists, because they always think Black people, when they see them out, are up to no good. We just sit on our porch, and they drive by real slow and give us dirty looks. They act like we got some disease or something. I don't see how they treat Whites, but I bet it is better than the way they treat me and my friends. We never did nothin' to them, they just think we are scum or something.

Respondent #6 - Yes the police are racist. They also treat people different because they are Black. I don't feel that way, but that is how most feel in my area. They say they are arrested because of who they are, not what they did. I say it's what they did.

Respondent #7 - Yes. It's like if three or more Black guys are hangin' on the corner, just out of school, gettin' off the bus, they'll pull up and harass them just because of stereotypes, thinkin' it's gotta be a gang. Or, four or more deep in a car, Black guys, they'll pull 'em over. It could be four kids goin' to Azars goin' to work, they'll pull 'em over. That's basically what I see.

Respondent #8 - Yeah. I here a lot of people say that. They say that lots of the killings go on, the police say that it's not ok for Blacks killin' Whites, but Whites kill Blacks or Whites kill Whites, it's ok. If a White person get killed justice is served right away. Also if a Black person kills another Black person in a black neighborhood, it's highly publicized, but if a White person kills a Black or anotherWhite person you don't here nothin' about it.

Respondent #9 - You mean racist as in treat Blacks differently? I don't know, maybe. If you're in my neighborhood, whether White or black, the police are going to stop you. If your White you're buying, if you're black you're dealin'. Usually, they just tell the White kid to go home. But, the Blacks are always questioned and harassed. I don't know if I believe all this, but I think it is the way most people in my neighborhood feel.

Respondent #10 - It is hard to say, I don't see many Whites around this area to see if they get treated differently. I don't think many of my hommies would know either. As for all cities, I think most people would agree that Blacks are harassed more. That's why so many brothers are in prison. I think most people would say that police watch for Blacks to commit more crimes, and follow more Blacks around waiting for them to sell drugs, or rob some store to buy dope. I think most cops think young black boys are dealing drugs.

2. Do you think women are treated differently by the police? Why, why not? Do you think Black women are treated differently than white Women by police?

Respondent #1 - No. If the woman act like a man, she gets treated the same by police. I imagine this is the same for white women. If they out beatin' people up, carryin' guns, and stealin', the police will probably dog them too. Yes, I think the police will dog you whether you are male or female, if they think you' causing trouble.

Respondent #2 - Maybe the police will give a young woman a break before a guy. Like if they get in trouble they might let a girl go, but not the guy. One time when I got stopped with my guy, he got busted and I didn't, and we was doin' the same thing. A lot of guys like to get young White girls into their gangs 'cause they can carry anything and never get bothered by the police. I don't think the police will ever hassle a White girl. Nothing personal, but I know some White girls that have done worse things than me, and they ain't never got in trouble.

Respondent #3 - Maybe police treat women different, I don't know. I've been in a lot more trouble than some of the guys I hang with, so I can't say for sure. But I know they don't hassle no White girls. I ain't never seen a white girl in juvenile, They always Black or Hispanic, and I know there are White girls sellin' and in gangs. Now I'm not trying to offend you, I'm just telling it the way I see it.

Respondent #4 - yes, females, especially White females are treated differently. I know of a case where the White girls committed the actual crime and my brothers are still in jail over it because they was with the girls. The girls were let go that day, my brothers are still in jail. They tryin' to waive my seventeen-year-old bother's case into adult court.

Respondent #5 - Yes, they treat girls differently. I know of a couple of incidence where my girlfriends got off for committing the same offense as the guys. It ain't fair, but I know it happens. As for White girls being treated differently, I can't say. I can't think of any examples.

Respondent #6 - The police are more sensitive toward women. They feel if women do something wrong it is for a reason. I don't think Black and White women get treated differently. I think that Black women are represented as being more violent and lazy, cause that's all the media shows. The media don't talk about what White women are doing.

Respondent #7 - All the time, never 'cause I did anything wrong, always 'cause I'm Black. No, because in my area, if they see a White person in my neighborhood, they'll get stopped too, because they can only be there 'cause they buying' or sellin' drugs. They're like the abnorm in the neighborhood, and they're like they gotta be down here buying'. They'll just stop 'em and ask 'em, what are you down here doin'? Women get treated differently by police, 'cause she can talk her way out of it, you know, a guy won't have much to say, but a female she can come up with about 100 different reason why she at the corner, the police always stoppin' women on that corner askin' them what they doin' on the corner and they usually just goin' to get milk and pampers or something. The police usually just let them slide, I don't think they are as harsh when it's a woman, Unless it's a female whose a known felon. Yeah, at the same time, me being from an interracial marriage, I can see it from both sides. I've seen both sides, and for a long time, I got treated differently because nobody, including me, knew where I belonged. Like I've seen the cops let a White girl go on Capital street and arrest the Black girls.

Respondent #8 - Yeah. Today I do, 'cause if you get in trouble in my neighborhood, you'll get arrested, it don't matter what color you are. If you in trouble, the law will stop you. They here to enforce the law. Women, I don't know? I might of got treated differently. I guess it depends on what you're involved in. If you sellin' or doin', they don't treat you any differently, but if you a prostitute, they usually don't mess with ya'. If you committing crimes, they'll walk all over you, but if you a respectable human being, they'll treat you with respect. No. not at all, Black and White women get treated the same in this area.

Respondent #9 - Maybe women get treated differently, I think maybe it depends on what the girls doin'. I think if you're selling drugs, the police are going to harass you whether you are male or female. It doesn't matter. Some other times they might let girls go, or not even consider them a suspect. White woman gettin' treated differently, I really don't know. I know the guys treat White women like they princesses or something. They get all protective of a White women comin' in the neighborhood. She might even be some white trash buying dope, but they give her respect. These same dude hate sisters who do drugs.

Respondent #10 - Women get treated differently 'cause the police think that they need to protect them. Most women I know can protect themselves. White women, I feel police think that they need even more protection.

D. Attitudes toward welfare:

1. Do most people in your area see welfare as necessary?

Respondent #1 - Yes, no one dogs anyone for tryin' to feed their kids. Most people can't find no jobs, the babies have to eat. Everyone knows this.

Respondent #2 - Yes, most mothers can't make it without welfare. No one makes fun of people on welfare anymore. They know it is something that is needed.

Respondent #3 - Yes, I don't think people blame anyone for collecting welfare. If it is something you need you just do it.

Respondent #4 - Yes, you get the money the best way you know how. A lot of women have babies so they can get welfare. But they have to quit after four, 'cause you get no additional money after the forth child.

Respondent #5 - Most collect welfare 'cause they got kids to feed. No one sees anything wrong with that. These kids got to eat somehow. There daddy's ain't sending them no money, and they can't find a job, so they do what they gotta do.

Respondent #6 - Yes welfare is necessary. If not on welfare most women would work in restaurant, as CNA's, or any other entry level job. Some people do abuse the welfare system, but most women use it to get ahead. Like me, I'm going to school and trying to become something so I can be a role model for my kids. When I get my degree I can get off welfare. I'm not going to work for minimum wage when I can stay home and spend time with my children.

Respondent #7 - In my neighborhood all the women I know are on, and I'll say all, only time it differs is when the girl has a baby under age, and then she on it under her mom. Other than that it is very necessary, 'cause that's what's supportin' their habit. All the drugs are sold at the first of the month. Very Necessary. Alternatives to welfare, if they said will give you food, but for everything else you got to work. But, they don't say that, either work or don't get. I mean I don't at this point, but if I was usin' and had children, I can't have children at this point, but if I could, I'd have four or five babies, because that's an easy way to keep your supply comin' in, you know at the first of the month you gettin' that check. And you can do whatever you want during the month, 'cause you know every month the government goin' to be there at your door with a paycheck for ya'. I lived in a house where that's all they did, have three or four kids and they would pay them to run drugs out of their house a couple of days and they could stay rent free the rest the month.

Respondent #8 - To a certain degree. See, with me, I got three children, and when I get them back. I don't intend to be on welfare, I can go out and work. But for those who can't, for those who need assistance, it's necessary. But, for those who can go out and get a job, I don't know why they should rely on welfare.

Respondent #9 - Most women in this area are collecting welfare and sellin' dope out of their houses. It is kind of dangerous when you got kids, so some they just live off their welfare checks. I don't know of any jobs around here for women were they can make as much money as they do sellin' crack. I think a lot of women be smart when they collect welfare 'cause they get all the benefits. Most women who work don't get any health insurance for their kids, so they just never take there kids to the doctor. If the kid gets sick they end up sellin' a little on the side anyways to pay the doctor bills. Most women in this neighborhood get welfare 'cause they care about feedin' and taking care of their kids. That's the only way to do it. Ain't nobody going to hire us for much more than minimum wage, and if they do, they say it's part time, work ya' forty hours a week, and don't give you any health care plan. Also, it cost a lot of money to have someone watch your kids while you're at work. If your dealin' or on welfare, the kids can stay with you.

Respondent #10 - Yeah. Most people think welfare is ok. Nobodies going to criticize someone for gettin' money and food stamps so that they can feed their kids. It's hard to find a job out there where they offer you any kind of money. Then when you do work you get treated like dirt. These people hire us for minimum wage and then think they can treat us like slaves. We're still human beings. Welfare, or sellin' drugs allows you to keep your self respect. People around here respect women for doin' what they can to feed their babies. Especially when everyone seems to be against them. White employers.

2. What are some alternatives to welfare in your neighborhood? Do most people feel that women on welfare could find some other source of income if they wanted to?

Respondent #1 - A lot of women are on welfare and sellin' drugs. Neither one pays high enough so they got to do both. Most women around here don't like to leave their children and go to work. They can't find work anyway.

Respondent #2 - No one can find a job in this neighborhood, especially if you got kids. You can't afford to pay someone to watch them. Most women around here collect welfare, and sell drugs for their man, 'cause he is to strung out to do it himself. This one chick supports her man's habit by sellin' drugs for him. How can he pay support, when she has to work to buy his drugs. It is sad, but no one blames women on welfare.

Respondent #3 - There isn't any work around here that pays enough to raise a family, you got to collect welfare. No, sellin' drugs is not seen as an alternative, but additional income on top of their welfare checks.

Respondent #4 - Most people get welfare 'cause there is no alternative. They get money the best way they know how.

Respondent #5 - Welfare is usually always collected, If women are sellin' drugs, they're still collecting their welfare checks. A lot of young chicks hide their cadillac on the days the social worker is stopping by, because if they don't the social worker know she prostituting' or sellin'. I think most women would much rather sell than prostitute. I think that would be the number one choice for an alternative to welfare.

Respondent #6 - Not anything that pays more than entry level pay. It makes more sense, if you have kids to collect welfare. No one blames anyone for being on welfare, only if they use it in the wrong way, and don't try to get ahead.

Respondent #7 - For females, prostitution, strong armed robberies, conning', people in my neighborhood are always lookin' for a victim. If you want to work, for example, I had no skills or nothin', but when I got clean and wanted to work, there was plenty of jobs, there are plenty of jobs, like restaurants, janitorial, McDonalds, if you want to work.

Respondent #8 - Yes. If you seek them, and also if you get the education. I just finished a program for court recording and administrative assistance. It just depends on the Black woman.

Respondent #9 - No. Well maybe, if you wanted to take a low paying job that you can't go anywhere with. Anyone can get a job. But no one wants to hire someone like me to do a job that has some responsibility, and pays well. I was in charge of at least ten brothers and sisters runnin' drugs. I had to take care of the money and weigh the dope. I can handle a little responsibility. In the real world you can't get no respect.

Respondent #10 - Yeah. anybody can find work, But, sellin' drugs pays more. You can work as a janitor, at a restaurant. I don't know, anywhere.

PERCEPTIONS OF THE NATURE OF SOCIETY:

A. Sexism in society:

1. Do you think that women get the same respect as men in or outside your neighborhood?

Respondent #1 - Younger girls gettin' treated wrong, many messing around having babies and ending up on welfare. But if you treat men with respect they treat you with respect. Sometimes people in this area act like men know everything, but things are changing. Women are gettin' more respect.

Respondent #2 - I think it is harder for girls to earn respect than guys. Guys just beat someone up, or carry a gun and they got respect. But girls, if they mess up, they get treated like a ho. You got to watch who you sell to and hang with when you're a girl, 'cause the guys will mark you as a ho and an easy fuck, and they'll try to take advantage of you. But as you get older you learn how to take care of the men, and they start treating you better.

Respondent #3 - If you treat guys with respect they'll respect you. A lot of girls get dogged 'cause they do stupid shit. But most the time girls get treated the same as guys.

Respondent #4 - Guys get more attention, and women do not get the same respect on jobs. Males have better opportunities. The bosses think 'cause they are guys they will do a better job. For example, I was job hunting with my boyfriend and they said they would hire me if the hired my boyfriend. Than when they hired us, they said they hired my boyfriend and I at the same time so he could train me. I had a high school diploma and he didn't, but they thought he would catch on quicker and be able to train me. When my boyfriend got fired, they never put me back on the schedule.

Respondent #5 - Yeah, I think girls are treated differently. I don't think they get as good of jobs. Most employers will hire guys first, 'cause they think they'll do a better job. Guys around here don't respect women much, I think it is because of all the rap music bashin' women. I listen to some of this music calling women bitches and ho's and it upsets me. I think the guys around here think sex is all we're good for. They'll use us when they want some, but they don't really give a shit about what happens to us after that.

Respondent #6 - No, they don't get the same respect. If a man does something, he thinks it is done right. If a woman does something, the man thinks he has to follow after her so it is done right, but the truth is, if a woman does it, it will probably be done right. Yes, society is prejudice against Black women, the media makes her out to be someone that don't do nothing. All society do is put them down.

This lowers Black women's self-esteem.

Respondent #7 - Definitely not! because as a girl, I got more respect by sellin' myself than if I did by just havin' a boyfriend outside the G's, but if a guy gives it away it's alright, but if a girl gives it away she is labeled as a slut or a ho. Now there's a difference between a whore and a slut. A ho get the money and a slut gives it away. And a women gets more respect if she chargin' and not just givin' it. If a women shows she deserves respect, she ain't goin' to get it without a fight, but she will get it.

Respondent #8 - Yeah.

Respondent #9 - I think women get respect if they earn it. Women who prostitute themselves, or have sex for drugs don't get any respect. But if you work, sell drugs, or get welfare to take care of your kids you get respect. I think girls have to work harder to get respect, but when they prove they're tough they get it. In gangs women who get beat in get more respect than those who have sex. Like if you a girl and you enter the gang the same way men do, by gettin' beat up you're a full member of that gang, just like the guys. But if you have sex with the gang members to join the gang, they'll always treat you with disrespect. like you a ho or something. You'll never get rid of that title.

Respondent #10 - Yeah. I think girls get lots of respect. The only girls not respected around here are the ones that are givin' it up for drugs, or are sellin' themselves to buy. Most women get respect if they sellin' drugs, but not if they are using. It's ok for guys to use, but not us.

2. Do you think women who sell drugs get the same respect as males that sell drugs?

Respondent #1 - If you have respect for others you get respect in return. I think some women get more respect, 'cause they are women who are tough, and don't take no shit off anybody.

Respondent #2 - I think a lot of times the women are just sellin' for their old man. If they are, then no one gives them much respect. But if they are sellin' for themselves I think they get as much respect as male dealers.

Respondent #3 - If they're makin' good money they get lots of respect. Just like the guys, if they make good money they earn respect.

Respondent #4 - Yes, I think so.

Respondent #5 - I think if you earn respect, you get it whether you are male or female. It don't matter. When you sellin' you get respect by makin' money and not letting anybody get over on you. If you do that you get respect, male or female.

Respondent #6 - No, if women would try to sell drugs, the males would try to take over and dominate her. They think they are the only ones who can do something right. No, they don't get as much respect.

Respondent #7 - yes, they can't be soft though, if they present themselves as strong enough to be in that trade, than they goin' to get the same respect, if not more so.

Respondent #8 - Yeah. She's out there with him ain't she? So, Yeah.

Respondent #9 - Yeah. Most women if they actin' like men get the same respect as men. It's the same as in legitimate businesses. Those women who act aggressive and will do anything to get to the top, get to the top, and get respect. Those women who sleep their way to the top, or are too soft, ain't goin' get the same respect.

Respondent #10 - Yeah. I think women, if they're tough, they get the same respect.

B. Racism in society:

1. Do you think people in your neighborhood are racists? Society as a whole racists? Do you think that black females have different experiences in life compared to white females?

Respondent #1 - Yeah, especially on the job. When you workin', they always watch you when your friends come in. They think your going to give your friends something extra. Think you gonna give away free food to your friends. Also, I can't walk down Coldwater, the police will stop me, ask me what I'm doin' and take me to jail. One time I was in a store and a county cop followed me all over the store. They think most black people always out stealing. You can't ever go to shows 'cause white people always lookin' at ya' funny. I don't think they treat white people this way. Especially white females.

Respondent #2 - Yeah, I think people are racist, because they always look at me funny, and think I'm going to rob them or beat them up. Everyone is scared of you if you Black. It is funny sometimes, but other times it hurts. I feel like people think Black females are all mean and loud. They look at us funny when we hang together trying to have a good time. If we get real loud they get all shitty. If there are a bunch of young White girls in the mall gettin' loud everyone thinks they cute, or ignores them. In that way I think Black girls get treated differently. I don't mean to offend you, but if you got loud, and was having fun, nobody would probably say nothing.

Respondent #3 - I think we get treated a little bit differently than White females. But I don't know, 'cause I don't know how you get treated. But it's like every time I go to the store with my friends the managers, or security are always following us around. Like they think 'cause we Black we couldn't afford to buy nothin' so we must be stealing. They always think Black people are going to steal something. I think Black girls have lower self-esteems 'cause they always treated like they're poor or on welfare. In that way I think they are treated differently than White girls.

Respondent #4 - Yeah. I think society is racist. For example, they kicked this black kid out of school, because he was defending himself from a White guy. They never even asked the Black guy his side of the story, or checked out the White guys story with other kids. They just kicked him out, 'cause he was Black, it must have been his fault. White and Black females? I really can't think of any differences. I guess we get treated the same. I don't know.

Respondent #5 - I think Blacks are treated differently. Everybody acts like they're scared of you. I think the media has a lot to do with these attitudes. They are always showing on the news, Black guys shooting each other over drugs. One time I know this White guy shot a Black guy and the news intentionally said the guy who shot the other guy was Black. It always makes me mad when the media makes Black guys look like murderers. I know they're a lot more White guys killing each other than the television tells us. If they are White, the news ain't going to print it, or they won't say a color. Like if a White guy kills someone they just talk about the murder, not the "White" guy killed another "White" guy. That's what they do if it is a Black kid killing someone. The headlines will read "a 17 year-old Black boy kills an innocent White man over a drug deal." I think that is racists. I think Black women get treated differently, 'cause they think we are violent like the Black men. I think White women are scared of us, like they are men. I don't mean to offend you, but that's what I think.

Respondent #6 - Some people in my neighborhood are racist. They don't think they can be racist, but they are. They say Whites and Mexicans are doing better than them because they have lighter skin, not because they pushed themselves to do better. Some aspects of society are racist. Like the people who are higher up in the ranks, they look down on us, because they think they are better than us. They shouldn't do that, because nobody is better than anyone else. They should stop putting people down and start helping people pull themselves up. The media focuses in on the Black female family being dysfunctional, violent and drug selling. This just generates false stereotypes about who we are.

Respondent #7 - Yeah, 'cause in my neighborhood, which is predominately Black, if a White person comes in, it's like what's this mother fucker want, yeah we goin' get him, or automatically then he's a sucker, and he goin' get beat. Yeah, like I'm on both sides of it. I go to my moms and it's niggah this and niggah that, and on my dads side it's honky this and honky that, and I'm just like where do I fit in? I had and identity crisis for a long time. The White children, in my opinion, show less respect for their parents, and in the Black family, even though they get less, they respect their parents. They see that the parents do what they can. Even though it's just a little they respect their parents for what they give them. When a White girl comes into the neighborhood, even if she with a Black guy, she gets treated like a premidonna, she gets more attention, and the Black girl basically has lower self-esteem 'cause of the way she treated. In the neighborhood where I live, they're some White girls usin', but because they White, no one thinks they're usin', but if they in that neighborhood everybodies usin'.

Respondent #8 - No. I don't see anything racist, or racism today? No. Black women don't experience anything different than White females.

Respondent #9 - Yeah. sometimes I think the police and other White folks are kinda scared or leery of Blacks. Maybe not you, but some of 'em. I think it's because the media always shows the Black guy that gets shot, or does the shooting, but they never talk about the White guys that kill. I think the only difference between White women and Black women is that I think it might be easier for a White women to get a job. I don't know, but I just see lots of young White girls workin'.

Respondent #10 - Maybe, it seems like everybody always plays Black folks as stupid or uneducated. I know lots of Black people are goin' to college, or have good jobs. Not all Black men are sellin' drugs. That's what most people think that the Blacks are sellin' the drugs. Blacks might be sellin' drugs, but we ain't the ones bringing' it in the neighborhood. I don't think there's much difference between Black and White females. Maybe White females, sometimes get treated like they're queens are something. Nothing personal, but a lot of times when brothers see a White women, they talk like she's something special. But I don't think they respect her.

C. Attitudes toward the legalization of drugs:

1. Do you think drugs should be legalized? If yes, all or some, why, why not?

Respondent #1 - Not all, maybe Bud (Marijuana). Not crack 'cause crack is killing people. How we gettin' drugs in here anyway? White people brings it in and Black people spread it out and kill one another. I think the Whites bringing the drugs in are trying to kill the blacks. You don't see to many wealthy Whites doin' crack, but they are making lots of money off bringing it into our neighborhoods.

Respondent #2 - Maybe all but Crack. Crack is killing everybody. I never done crack, but what is does to people is sad. It kills them. They get so addicted they become like a vegetable or something.

Respondent #3 - Yeah, but no crack, it's too dangerous! I have seen people addicted to crack, and they look pretty bad. They would sell their own children for crack if they had too. A lot of women out there selling sex to get a rock. it is running down our neighborhoods.

Respondent #4 - Legalizing would only make things worse, 'cause people would be doing drugs out in the open. Might as well though, 'cause you can't stop everyone from doing them. If you made drugs legal the world would come to an end. They even sell pills to get drugs out of your system by the next day, for those who have to take drug tests.

Respondent #5 - If they made drugs legal, maybe people in the inner-cities could have legitimate jobs. Selling drugs seems to be all they are qualified to do. They would be the perfect job applicants when drugs became legal. But if drugs became legal, selling them would probably become a minimum wage job.

Respondent #6 - No, if you legalize drugs it will cause more harm than what has already been done. Blacks sell drugs, but all different kinds of people bring drugs into our neighborhoods.

Respondent #7 - definitely not, 'cause things are crazy enough. On drugs you just lose everything, and most of all you lose yourself. There should be some gratitude for the handful of us who is out here and kicked the habit, 'cause if everybody was out there using like I was when I was usin' then it would be crazy. It would be insane, that would be total genocide. That would be killin' the human race if you legalized them. No drugs should be legal, not even nicotine, caffeine.

Respondent #8 - No. no drugs at all

Respondent #9 - No. No drugs at all, not even alcohol.

Respondent #10 - No. Well, maybe marijuana. Definitely not crack. That stuff is dangerous. People get stupid on that shit.

D. Attitudes Toward the Future:
1. What do you see yourself doing in ten years?

Respondent #1 - I haven't thought much about the future. I take things one day at a time.

Respondent #2 - I don't know, I haven't thought much about it. Maybe I'll be married, have a couple of children, and a husband.

Respondent #3 - Maybe I'll go back to school. I need an education to do what I want to do. I would like to be a nurse. I think nurses get a lot of respect and make good money. I don't know, maybe I'll just get married and raise a family.

Respondent #4 - Married, with a nice home, nice job, maybe a cosmetologist, or child care, or computers. My mother tells me I would be good with computers.

Respondent #5 - Maybe I'll be teaching school. I would like to go back to be a teacher, grade school, High school teachers don't get any respect. It's too late by high school.

Respondent #6 - I see myself with a Master's degree in computer science, maybe own my own company, children grown, secure, educated, living a comfortable life.

Respondent #7 - an everyday workin' class girl, being comfortable, lookin' for a little more inner peace within myself.

Respondent #8 - I hope to be a court recorder, or working as a counselor at an addictions center. Because, I went through treatment and people helped me, and I want to help others. People helped me believe I wasn't hopeless when I thought I was, and I want to give that back to someone or give back to the community in that way.

Respondent #9 - maybe I'll go to beauty school. I have a friend that runs a hairdressing shop, and she's doin' pretty good for herself. I'll probably have kids, be married.

Respondent #10 - I want to eventually go to school to study nursing. I always thought that would be cool to work with sick people, and make them better. Maybe I'll have a family. I would like to have a bunch of kids. I love kids.

2. What do you see your friends doing in ten years?

Respondent #1 - They like life the way it is. The way life is you barely think about something good happening.

Respondent #2 - I don't know, most of them will probably be dead or in prison. Most the people around here don't make much of themselves. Even if they have dreams, they never reach them, they usually start using drugs, or get shot 'cause they dealing.

Respondent #3 - Most will be in prison or dead. It's hard, even if you want to go to college, or whatever, it seems like the streets hold you back. You always keep goin' back to street life. It's seems like the only thing that feels comfortable. When you get outside the 'hood things are scary.

Respondent #4 - Working, a lot who were in gangs grew out of them, a lot don't make it to an age to grow out of it. My Brother by the age 20 will probably be in prison, my youngest brother, the same place. A lot of my friends are locked up or dead. It is hard to get out today.

Respondent #5 - I think some will probably make it. like I got one friend who is goin' to IPFW [Indiana-Purdue, Fort Wayne]. He is doin' real good in school and he stop sellin'. His friends dog him a lot, but he knows what he wants to do. He is hoping to get good enough grades so he can get a scholarship and transfer down to the Bloomington campus [Indiana University].

Respondent #6 - I hope they will be doing the same thing I am. Our children have the strength to pull themselves out of this. All we adults have to do is show them the right way so they have the materials to use the right way to pull themselves up.

Respondent #7 - If they usin' or not usin'? If they are using they'll probably be dead, if not I see them the same place I expect to be.

Respondent #8 - A lot of people I see are goin' to be productive members of society, but the ones on drugs, I can't say right now. I hope they're not dead, but that's what it looks like.

Respondent #9 - Maybe move out of the neighborhood, stop dealin' or doin' drugs. If they don't they're going to be dead or in prison.

Respondent #10 - Some of them will probably make something of themselves, go to college. The rest will be dead or in prison. It's sad.

BIBLIOGRAPHY

Abramowitz, S. I. (1982). The sexual politics of sex bias in psycho-therapy research. *Micropolitics, 2*(1), 21-34.

Andersen, M. (1993). Studying across difference: Race, class, and gender in qualitative research. In J. H. Stanfield, II, & R. M. Dennis (Eds.), *Race and ethnicity in research* (pp. 39-52). Newbury Park, CA: Sage.

Anderson, E. (1990). *Street wise*. Chicago, IL: University of Chicago Press.

Andreas, P. (1990). U.S. drug policy and Andean narcoeconomic realities. In A. S. Trebach, & K. B. Zeese (Eds.), *New frontiers in drug policy* (pp. 159-164). Washington, DC: The Drug Policy Foundation.

Asbury, H. (1969). *Sucker's progress: An informal history of gambling in America from the colonies to Canfield*. Monclair, NJ: Patterson Smith.

Baldwin, J. (1962). *Nobody knows my name*. New York: Dell Publications.

Beirne, P., & Messerschmidt, J. (1991). *Criminology*. New York: Harcourt, Brace, Jovanovich.

Bernick, S.E. (1991). Toward a value-laden theory: Feminism and social science. *Hypatia, 6*, 118-136.

Bowker, L. H.; Gross, H. S.; & Klein, M. W. (1980). Female participation in delinquent gang activities. *Adolescence, 14* (59), 509-519.

Brown, R. M. (1990). The black community and the war on drugs. In A. Trebach, & K. B. Zeese (Eds.), *The great issues of drug policy* (pp. 83-87). Washington, DC: The Drug Policy Foundation.

Brown, W. K. (1977). Black female gangs in Philadelphia. *International Journal of Offender Therapy and Comparative Criminology, 21*, 221-228.

Campbell, A. (1984). *The girls in the gang*. New York: Basil Blackwell.

Christman, J. B. (1988). Working in the field as the female friend. *Anthropology and Education Quarterly, 19* (2), 70-85.

Cloward, R. A., & Ohlin, L. E. (1960). *Delinquency and opportunity: A theory of delinquent gangs*. New York: Free Press.

Collins, P.H. (1990). *Black feminist thought: Knowledge, consciousness and the politics of empowerment*. New York: Routledge.

Cooper, A. J. (1988). *A voice from the south*. New York: Oxford University Press. (Original work published 1892)

Currie, D. (1988). Rethinking what we do and how we do it: A study of reproductive decisions. *Canadian Review of Sociology and Anthropology, 25,* 231-253.

Currie, E. (1989). *Dope and trouble*. New York: Pantheon Books.

Davis, A. Y. (1981). *Women, race & class*. New York: Random House. (Original work published 1944).

Denzin, N. K., & Lincoln, Y. S. (1994). *Handbook of qualitative research*. Thousand Oaks, CA: Sage.

Devault, M. L. (1990). Talking and listening from women's standpoint: Feminist strategies for interviewing and analysis. *Social Problems, 37,* 96-116.

Ellison, R. (1947). *Invisible man*. New York: Random House.

Ellison, R. (1964). *Shadow and act*. New York: Random House.

Fishman, L. (1988, October). *The vice queens: An ethnographic study of black female gang behavior*: Paper presented at the annual meeting of the American Society of Criminology, Chicago, IL.

Fort Wayne Data Book. (1993). Fort Wayne Chamber of Commerce and The City of Fort Wayne Economic Development.

Goode, E. (1989). *Drugs in American society*. New York: McGraw-Hill.

Gouldner, A. W. (1970). *The coming crisis of western sociology*. New York: Basic Books

Grant, L., & Ward, K. (1987). Is there an association between gender and in sociological research? *American Sociological Review, 52*, 856-862.

Harris, A. P. (1990). Race and essentialism in feminist legal theory. In K. T. Barlett, & R. Kennedy (Eds.), *Feminist legal theory: Readings in law and gender* (pp. 235-262). Boulder, CO: Westview Press.

Harris, L. (1992). Agency and the concept of the underclass. In B. E. Lawson (Ed.), *The underclass question* (pp. 33-54). Philadelphia, PA: Temple University Press.

Harris, M. G. (1988). *Cholas: Latino girls and gangs.* New York: AMS.

hooks, b. (1981). *Ain't I a woman.* Boston, MA: South End Press.

Horowitz, R. (1983). *Honor and the American dream: Culture and identity in the Chicano community.* New Brunswick, NJ: Rutgers University Press.

Huff, C. R. (1990). *Gangs in America.* Newbury Park, CA: Sage

Jaffee, D. (1990). *Handbook of Monetary Economics.* New York: North-Holland.

Jankowski, M. S. (1991). *Islands in the street.* Berkeley, CA: University of California Press.

Kirkland, F. M. (1992). Social policy, ethical life, and the urban underclass. In B. E. Lawson (Ed.), *The underclass question* (pp. 152-190). Philadelphia, PA: Temple University Press.

Kitchen, D. B., & Davidson, D. V. (1993, October) (A critical look at perspectives on drug related gang violence). Paper presented at the annual meeting of the American Society of Criminology, Boston, MA.

Kitchen, D. B.; Davidson, D. V.; & Walker, L. (1994, March). *Reflections on race, class, and violence: The continuing American dilemma.* Paper presented at the annual meeting of the Midwest Sociological Association, Saint Louis, MO.

Kozol, J. (1991). Savage Inequalities: Children in America's Schools. New York: Crown Publication.

Lather, P. (1986). Issues and validity in openly ideological research: Between a rock and a soft place. *Interchange*, *17*(4) 63-84

Lawson, B. (1992). *The Underclass Question*. Philadeplphia: Temple University Press.

Leiman, M. M. (1993). *Political economy of racism*. Boulder, CO: Pluto Press.

Lyman, M. (1989). *Gangland: Drug trafficking by organized criminals*. Springfield, IL: Charles C. Thomas.

MacKinnon, C. A. (1982). Feminism, marxism, methods, and the state: An agenda for theory. *Signs*, *7*, 515-544.

Malveaux, J. (1985). The economic interests of black and white women: Are they the same? *The Review of the Black Political Economy*, *14*, 5-27.

Marburg, S. L. (1981, April). *Paradigms of production: Theoretical basis for bias? A history of the idea man's role, woman's place in geography*. Paper Presented at the annual meeting of the Association of American Geographers, Los Angeles, CA.

Martin, J. M., & Romano, A. T. (1992). *Multinational crime: Terrorism, espionage, drug and arms trafficking*. Newbury Park, CA: Sage.

Mascia-Lees, F.E.; Sharpe, P.; & Cohen, C. B. (1989). The postmodernist turn in anthropology: Cautions from a feminist perspective. *Signs*, *15*, 7-33.

McCrea, F. & Markle, G. *Minutes to midnight: Nuclear weapons protest in America*. Newbury Park, CA. Sage.

McKegancy, N., & Bloor, M. (1991). Spotting the invisible man: The influence of male gender on fieldwork relations. *British Journal of Sociology*, *42*, 195-210.

Merton, R. K. (1938). Social structure and anomie. *The American Sociological Review*, *3*, 672-682.

Merton, R. K. (1957). *Social theory and social structure* Glencoe, IL: The Free Press.

Messner, S. F., & Rosenfeld, R. (1994). *Crime and the American dream.* Belmont, CA: Wadsworth.

Miller, W. B. (1958). Lower class culture as a generating milieu of gang delinquency. *Journal of Social Issues, 14*(3), 5-19.

Miller, W. B. (1973). The molls. *Society, 11,* 32-35.

Miller, W. B. (1975, November). *Violence by youth gangs and youth groups as a crime problem in major American cities.* Report to the National Institute for Juvenile Justice and Delinquency Prevention.

Moraga, C. & Gloria Anzaldua. (1981). *This Bridge Called My Back: Writings by Radical Women of Color.* Watertown, Mass: Persephone Press.

Moyers, B. (1986). A CBS report: The vanishing family-crisis in black America. A CBS Documentary.

Moynihan, D. P. (1965). Employment, income and the ordeal of the negro family. In T. Parsons, & K. B. Clark (Eds.), *The Negro American* (pp. 79-104). Boston: Beacon Press.

Musto, D. F. (1973). *The American Disease: Origins of narcotic control.* New Haven, CN: Yale Press.

Peplau, L. A., & Conrad, E. (1989). Beyond non sexist research: The perils of feminist in psychology. *Psychology of Women Quarterly, 13,* 379-400.

Pfohl, S. (1994). *Images of deviance and social control: A sociological history* (2nd ed.). New York: McGraw-Hill.

Portes, A., & Walton, J. (1981). *Labor, Class and the International System.* New York: Academic Press.

Prothrow-Smith, D. (1991). *Deadly Consequences*: New York: Harpar Collins.

Quicker, J. C. (1983). *Homegirls: Characterizing Chicano gangs*. San Pedro, CA: International University Press.

Rapp, R. (1988). Is the legacy of second wave feminism postmodernism? *Socialist Review, 18*, 31-37

Rice, R. (1963). A report at large: The Pursain queens. *New Yorker, 39*(35), 153.

Rollins, J. (1985). *Between women: Domestics and their employers*. Philadelphia, PA: Temple University Press.

Samaha, J. (1994). *Criminal justice* (3rd ed.). New York: West.

Sifakis, C. (1987). *The Mafia Encylopedia*. New York: Facts on File.

Simms, M. C. (1985). Black women who head families: An economic struggle. *The review of the black political economy, 14*, 141-151

Sowell, T. (1984). *Civil rights: Rhetoric or reality*. New York: William Morrow.

Sparr, P. (1984, September). Re-evaluating feminist economics. *Dollars and Sense*, pp. 15-21.

Sprague, J., & Zimmerman, M. K. (1989). Quality and quantity: Reconstructing feminist methodology. *American Sociologist, 20*, 71-86.

Stanfield, J. H. II. (1993). Epistemological considerations. In J. H. Stanfield, II, & R. M. Dennis (Eds.), *Race and ethnicity in research* (pp. 16-36). Newbury Park, CA: Sage.

Sudarkasa, N. (1986). In a world of women: Field work in a toruba community. In P. Golde (Ed.), *Women in the field: Anthropological experiences* (pp. 47-64). Berkeley, CA: University of California Press.

Taylor, C. S. (1990). *Dangerous society*. East Lansing, MI: Michigan State University Press.

Taylor, C. S. (1993). *Girls, gangs, women and drugs*. East Lansing, MI: Michigan State University Press.

Thomas, J. J. (1992). *Informal economic activity*. Ann Arbor, MI: The University of Michigan Press.

Thomas, J. (1993). *Doing critical ethnography*. Newbury Park, CA: Sage.

Thrasher, F. (1927). *The gang*. Chicago, IL: University of Chicago Press.

ULI-The Urban Land Institute. (1990). A panel advisory service report. Washington, DC.

U.S. Bureau of the Census. (1991). *Statistical abstract of the United States: 1991*. Washington, DC: U.S. Government Printing Office.

U.S. Commission on Civil Rights. (1983). *A growing crisis: Disadvantaged women and their children*. Washington, DC: Clearinghouse Publication.

Wallace, M. (1990). *Invisibility blues: From pop to theory*. New York: Verso.

Warren, C. A. B. (1988). *Gender issues in field research.*. Newbury Park, CA: Sage.

Weisheit, R. A. (1990). Declaring a civil war on drugs. In R. Weisheit (Eds.), *Drugs, crime and the criminal justice system* (pp. 1-10). Cincinnati, OH: Anderson Publishing.

West, R. (1988). *Jurisprudence and gender*. Chicago, IL: University of Chicago Press.

Whyte, W. F. (1943). *Street corner society*. Chicago, IL: University of Chicago Press.

Williams, A. (1987). Reading feminism in fieldnotes. *Studies in Sexual Politics, 16*, 100-109.

Williams, A. (1990). Reflections on the makings of an ethnographic text. *Studies in Sexual Politics, 29*, 1-63.

Williams, T. (1989). *The cocaine kids: The inside story of a teenage drug ring*. New York: Addison-Wesley.

Williams, T. (1992). *Crackhouse*. New York: Penguin Books.

Wilson, N. K. (1993). Stealing and dealing: The drug war and gendered criminal opportunity. In C. C. Culliver (Ed.) *Female criminality: The state of the art* (pp. 169-194). New York & London: Garland Publishing Company.

Wilson, W. J. (1987). *The truly disadvantaged.* Chicago, IL: University of Chicago Press.

INDEX

WOMEN'S STUDIES